ACTIVITY-BASED MANAGEMENT: ARTHUR ANDERSEN'S LESSONS FROM THE ABM BATTLEFIELD

SHARON MUNGER
Chief Executive Officer, The M/A/R/C Group

"Gaining and maintaining a competitive edge in today's marketplace is harder than ever before. *Activity-Based Management* effectively leverages the desire for responsive, lasting change with the need for credible, affordable resources. This book sets a new standard in the industry and for the transformations occurring in corporate America. Everyone should read it."

STEVE ROBBINS
Controller, Hewlett-Packard, North American Distribution Organization

"When I saw the results from our activity-based management project, I felt like the man who discovered the microscope. The information has always been there, but with these tools and the knowledge and leadership available through Arthur Andersen, I am able to see it. The results are dramatic.

"Arthur Andersen provides a depth of experience unsurpassable in the industry. By securing knowledgeable professionals with a unique team approach, the firm is able to demystify the world of cost management. This book represents the culmination of decades of industry and professional leadership."

TONY SPIRITO
Activity-Based Management Manager, Digital Equipment Corporation

"*Arthur Andersen's Lessons from the ABM Battlefield* clearly demonstrates that activity-based management is the foundation for any competitiveness initiative, whether focused on cost, quality, or time. It sets the standard for providing insight into how to make change happen and delivers the tools on how to sustain it."

GEORGE FOSTER
Paul L. and Phyllis Wattis Professor of Management
Stanford School of Business

"*Lessons from the ABM Battlefield* is a rich source of insights into the many opportunities with ABM. It highlights in a readable and powerful way the often-encountered roadblocks to successful ABM implementation."

RICK FINKBEINER
Senior Vice President, NordicTrack

"Arthur Andersen's team possesses the knowledge to manage costs and take the cost out of business by providing cutting edge insights into advanced cost management. *Activity-Based Management* transforms the way we view cost management from the development stage to the actual implementation. This book is filled with vital and practical tools for change.

"Arthur Andersen exceeds the industry standards with this comprehensive book that details the often untold cost management projects— the ones that fail. By detailing the pitfalls and how to overcome them, companies are able to successfully manage costs for the future."

BARRY BRINKER
Editor, *The Journal of Cost Management*

"This book provides an invaluable service: it explains how ABM can transform the way companies manage costs by enhancing revenue, reducing costs, increasing productivity, decreasing waste, and improving efficiency. But the book also does something that few competing books have done by pointing out the many pitfalls in implementing ABM and showing how to avoid them. The book thus provides a significant addition to the literature."

FRANKLIN SMITH
Controller, Johnson Controls

"Steve Player and his team provide Cost Management expertise with an innovative cross-industry perspective. By focusing their broad-based knowledge capital, they ensure clients in every industry realize significant and pervasive results. Executives at every level will benefit from their leading edge vision."

EDWARD McPHERSON
President, The InterSolve Group

"*Activity-Based Management* contributes toward understanding the transformation occurring in corporate America."

DICK MISKE
Manager, Global Manufacturing & Engineering, AT&T

"Arthur Andersen provides a unique learning opportunity enabling a high level of understanding and breakthrough results in a surprisingly short time frame. Details, densely packed in a diverse set of case studies, are the key. These 'lessons' set this book apart from many of the others that fill your bookshelf."

ACTIVITY-BASED MANAGEMENT

Arthur Andersen's Lessons from the ABM Battlefield

Edited by

Steve Player & David E. Keys

 **MASTERMEDIA LIMITED**

New York

Published by MasterMedia Limited

MASTERMEDIA and colophon are registered trademarks
of MasterMedia Limited.

    p.   cm.
ISBN 1-57-101-054-8: $24.95

                     95-080259
                     CIP

Designed by Virginia Koenke Hunt
Manufactured in the United States of America

DEDICATION

*We dedicate this book to Lydia, David, Emily, and Cole Player and
Diana Keys. This book could not have been completed without
their support and patience. Their love and understanding sustains
and encourages us to victory on any battlefield.*

ACKNOWLEDGEMENTS

We gratefully acknowledge the assistance and input of the Consortium for Advanced Manufacturing–International's (CAM–I) Cost Management System Program. In particular, the ABM Experience Interest Group; Peter Zampino, Program Manager of CAM–I; and Gary Cokins of EDS, former Chairman of the ABM Experience Interest Group.

In addition, we thank the clients of Arthur Andersen who participated in this research project. Their willingness to share not only their successes but also their pains, their frustrations, and the lessons they learned have made this book possible.

Thanks to Merrie Spaeth of Spaeth Communications, Inc., for helping us decide to do the book in the first place, and to Susan Stautberg, Melinda Lombard, Hedy F. Campbell, and Virginia Koenke Hunt of MasterMedia for their patience and diligence in turning our words into this product.

Thanks also goes to Barry Brinker, executive editor of *Journal of Cost Management*, for his very helpful comments on the chapters in Section 1, to Mary Trijiani of SPADA, Chuck Marx, Chuck Ketteman, and Steve Hronec of Arthur Andersen for their suggestions in improving the drafts, and to Sondra Green and Jeri Turner of Arthur Andersen for their logistical support. Special thanks goes to Paige Dawson of Spaeth Communications, Inc., for coordinating and expediting the publication of the text. Without her driving persistence, this book may never have been completed.

We also acknowledge the members of Arthur Andersen's Advanced Cost Management Team for taking the time to capture and contribute the lessons they have learned. We appreciate the significant contributions made by: David M. Aldea, Joseph W. Bagan, Jason Balogh, David E. Bullinger, Craig R. Collins, Jay Collins, Robert G. Cummiskey, Reid Dalton, John J. Dutton, Ellen Fitzpatrick, Terrence B. Hobdy, Michael B. Kramer, Billie Gayle Lewis, Chuck Marx, Joe McNeely, Angela A. Minas, Mark A. Moelling, Richard Storey, Robert C. Thames, John F. Vale, and Cathie Wier.

TABLE OF CONTENTS

Section III

Future Weapons: The Next Wave of Lessons

Appendices

FOREWORD

Since writing *The 7 Habits of Highly Effective People* and the follow-up books, *Principle-Centered Leadership* and *First Things First*, I've seen literally millions of people and thousands of organizations experience serious improvements in their effectiveness by focusing on principles and the character ethic. But, as I observe this, particularly over time, I am often concerned that people only see a portion of the message.

Management techniques in recent decades have been so heavily skewed toward the personality ethic and heavy authoritarian control that many readers and listeners are left feeling trapped in a lose/win, work-centered relationship with their organizations. Many have a deep thirst for a principle-centered work and personal life that brings them to a more balanced, harmonious way of living.

These seemingly competitive forces — demand for business results on the one hand, and the need for a rich, satisfying personal and family life and a positive, supportive professional environment on the other — have set in motion a massive corporate motivational pendulum. This pendulum swings to the traditional heavy-handed control approach that forces results. But then it responds to the resulting low morale and declining productivity by swinging over to the soft, permissive approach, only to then come crashing right back through the wall to authoritarian win/lose because management has the sense they're losing control and moving toward chaos. With these continual pendulum shifts, the culture is consumed in constantly surveying the political winds and becoming increasingly cynical and fatigued. Then decision-making is more reliant on the current read of the mood in the executive offices than it is on real information.

On the surface, Principle-Centered Leadership and the 7 Habits are sometimes viewed and written off as a soft, touchy-feely approach that has no regard for real bottom-line issues. Nothing could be further from the truth. Those looking deeper will find that principle-centered leadership is an approach that is not only kinder, but much tougher and results-oriented.

Similarly, some might make the mistake of seeing Arthur Andersen's activity-based management (ABM) system as a technical, narrow focus on accounting and costs. Both kinds of thinking remind me of the longstanding debate between leadership and management. Is it visionary leadership or is it rigorous management that produces a healthy, growing, profitable enterprise? The fact is that no organization is going to survive and thrive without real strength in both areas.

Those who look deeply into the process of activity-based management will find that it is an area of management that will empower them with the solid information about their organizations that *enables* them to exercise leadership and wisdom in decision making. As Max DePree taught, "The first responsibility of a leader is to define reality." ABM is not just more theory. It points with laser clarity to the practical. ABM gives you the operational guts to meet the leadership challenge and to see and seize your opportunities.

Because we at Covey Leadership Center have focused so much on the leadership dimension, we've needed this kind of management strength and insight. We've needed to more deeply understand the relative costs and value of our activities. We are obtaining it by implementing an activity-based management system with the assistance of Arthur Andersen. It is helping enormously.

These *Lessons from the ABM Battlefield* provide not only vital tools, but also key insights into the painful pitfalls others have made and how we can avoid them. They will be powerfully helpful to either those just beginning the process, or those on the ABM battlefield trying to get back on the right track.

There is tremendous strength in seeing and understanding the *details* that this process provides. They enable one to step back and holistically see in context *all* organizational activities — both leadership and management. In a sense, it answers a vital piece of one of *the* great leadership questions: "Is the ladder we're all climbing leaning against the right wall?"

STEPHEN R. COVEY

INTRODUCTION

Activity-based management—ABM—is a management strategy that's making its mark in the competitive arena. Using ABM, many companies have won big victories over misallocation and misinformation. ABM is winning the war between mismanagement and strategic leadership—but many of the companies seeking to apply ABM are losing some major battles.

We decided it was high time to record the reasons why ABM is winning—and to explore the root cause of the losses. We studied independent research conducted by Arthur Andersen and the Consortium for Advanced Manufacturing–International (CAM–I). We evaluated the frontline implementations as experienced by Arthur Andersen's Advanced Cost Management Team. We also conducted more than 100 interviews with people who are implementing ABM, people who use the information ABM generates, consultants and even people who reject it as a management tool. Thirty of the interviews were conducted with members of CAM–I's Cost Management Systems ABM Experience Interest Group.

The result is this book designed to give the reader access to strategies and practical tips for deploying ABM. *Lessons from the ABM Battlefield* helps the reader understand what kind of an organization should implement ABM, how a company can implement ABM effectively, and how ABM can link with other improvement initiatives to really enhance a company's management performance. The first section consists of three chapters and synthesizes what we discovered about initiating ABM, developing a pilot, and converting that pilot into the mainstream systems of a company. The second section features 12 case studies that illustrate the successful implementation of ABM and activity-based costing, or ABC. These studies come directly from the multi-industry experiences of Arthur Andersen's Advanced Cost Management Team. The third section of the book covers advanced cost management issues.

2 ACTIVITY-BASED MANAGEMENT

We believe the results of this work deliver up some valuable lessons for any company thinking about ABM, about to start ABM, or recovering from a failure with ABM. And we've learned that the long-term success of ABM—like any new management method—depends on how well everyone in the organization understands both the benefits and risks of deploying ABM. We hope our views on the pitfalls that impede successful implementation of ABM help the reader and that by book's end, you'll be as convinced as we are that ABM can be a key weapon in today's competitive battlefield.

STEVE PLAYER
DAVID E. KEYS

Section I

The 30 Pitfalls of ABM and How to Overcome Them

I

GETTING OFF TO THE RIGHT START

STEVE PLAYER AND DAVID E. KEYS

There is an old saying: "How fast you are going is not as important as making sure you are on the right road." This is especially true in understanding the management of costs and how to implement activity-based management (ABM).

Five to seven years ago, many companies were trying to grasp the elements of activity-based costing (ABC). Today, many have had some experience— often painful or frustrating. A food processor on the Gulf Coast has abandoned its ABC effort because it took the model eight hours to update. A hospital goods manufacturer produces ABC reports but the operational personnel are not interested.

In many companies like these, an ABM pilot proves interesting but fails to move forward. Implementation teams are left to try and determine what went wrong. (Note: We have chosen to omit the specific company names in each of these examples because the related project teams have already suffered enough.)

While this could happen with your ABM project, we are here to report that the number of successful implementations is growing. Implementation teams are even receiving compliments, like those given to the Hewlett-Packard North American Distribution Organization teams by Controller Steve Robbins: "... I felt like the man who discovered the microscope. The information has always been there ... now I am able to see it."

Furthermore, CEOs are being converted and are speaking out about ABM. R.A. Pritzker, president of The Marmon Group, a $5 billion association of 65 manufacturing and service companies operating worldwide, says, "ABM has

4

done more in the past two years for our companies' understanding their costs than I have been able to achieve in the last 40 years." Companies are using ABM to reengineer operations (see Pennzoil), improve benchmarking (see AT&T), and increase revenues (see TTI, Inc.). Many are approaching this on a worldwide basis (see American Express).

To understand the process that will lead you to success and avoid any of the pitfalls that lead to failure, we begin with a definition of ABM and ABC. (Note: All definitions are taken from the CAM-I Glossary of Terms Version 1.2 in the attached glossary.)

Activity-based costing (ABC) is a methodology that measures the cost and performance of activities, resources, and cost objects. Resources are assigned to activities, then activities are assigned to cost objects based on their use. ABC recognizes the causal relationships of cost drivers to activities.

Activity-based management (ABM) is the broad discipline that focuses on achieving customer value and company profit via the management of activities. It draws on activity-based costing (ABC) as a major source of information.

When we refer to ABC in this book we are usually describing the use of activity analysis to improve the costing process. While ABC is typically used to determine product costs, it is equally applicable to determining customer costs, channel costs, etc. ABC focuses on determining "what things cost."

Benefits typically derived from ABC include:

- more accurate product costs;
- determination of the costs of services;
- determination of customer costs;
- identification of market or distribution channel costs;
- determination of project costs;
- determination of contract costs;
- determination of what products, customers, or channels to emphasize;
- tracking of direct mail catalog profitability;
- support for measurement of economic value analysis;
- support for contract negotiations;
- support for increasing revenue by helping customers understand their cost reductions through use of your products and services;
- support for target costing;
- support for benchmarking; and
- determination of shared services charge-out amounts.

The broader use of activity-based approaches inherent in ABM revolves around using activity-based information to manage operations. ABM focuses more on "how to change and improve your costs."

Benefits typically derived from ABM include:

- identification of redundant costs;
- analysis of value added and non-value added costs;
- quantification of the cost of quality by element;
- identification of customer focused activities;
- analysis of the cost of complexity;
- identification of process costs and support of process analysis;
- measurement of the impact of reengineering efforts;
- better understanding of cost drivers;
- evaluation of manufacturing flexibility investments; and
- activity-based budgeting.

While both ABC and ABM are new terms, their underlying techniques have a long history. A detailed methodology using an activity-based approach is found in *Improving Productivity and Profits in Wholesale Distribution—The Magnifying Glass Technique* by Arthur Andersen Partners Robert L. Grottke and James W. Norris, which was published in 1981 by the Distribution Research and Education Foundation. Similar concepts are discussed by Professor George J. Staubus in his book *Activity Costing and Input-Output Accounting*, which was published in 1971 by Richard D. Irwin, Inc. In his book *Relevance Regained*, Professor Tom Johnson traces the roots of many of these approaches used by General Electric in the 1960s. Finally, an activity-based management approach was addressed by Peter Drucker as early as 1954 when he noted that the way you manage an enterprise is by managing its activities.

With all of this history, we can wonder why it took this long to begin to see broad-scale applications of ABM. It is helpful to remember that Drucker also noted that it historically takes 35 years for an innovation to move into widespread use. So if we use Drucker's time frame, ABM's time has come.

For those of you who want to see the principles of ABM deliver results in less than 35 years, we can offer hope through the case studies in our second section. But first, it's best to know up front what could go wrong. We begin with the internal sell.

In analyzing ABM projects, numerous comments were focused on how to get projects off to the right start. The pitfalls encountered can be easily grouped by the direct comments from implementation teams. These have been grouped and summarized in Exhibit 1–1.

Exhibit 1–1

Pitfalls in Getting Off to the Right Start

Pitfall #1	"We can't get the top guys to buy it."
Pitfall #2	"Okay, tell me again why we're doing this."
Pitfall #3	"What do you mean, there are three views of cost?"
Pitfall #4	"Let's put the controller in charge."
Pitfall #5	"We'll tell the employees about this later—maybe."
Pitfall #6	"We can do this without spending any money."
Pitfall #7	"We don't need training—this isn't brain surgery."
Pitfall #8	"It's the consultant's fault."
Pitfall #9	"We don't need resident experts."
Pitfall #10	"This doesn't link to other initiatives."

Pitfall #1: "We can't get the top guys to buy it."

The decision to begin any improvement effort usually takes time. The way that many executives approach change has a great deal to do with how they endorse and implement new management initiatives. It helps to understand how most executives "get to" change; this is depicted in Exhibit 1–2.

Exhibit 1–2

Arthur Andersen's Awareness, Buy-In, Ownership (ABO) Continuum^{SM}

Awareness
Executives know something important is happening, and they show interest in it. Managers seek to learn more about the proposed change, attend meetings, and challenge traditional methods.

Buy-In
Executives begin to take personal responsibility for the change. They are willing to commit time, people, and money to the change. Executives begin to implement the change and communicate the benefits of the change to other people in the organization.

Ownership
Executives assume ultimate responsibility for the change. Managers recruit others to help apply and teach new concepts, and initiate efforts to continue the process of change.

The ABO Continuum^{SM}[1] alludes to the number-one pitfall in ABM projects: lack of top management buy-in from the get-go. In our research, this was the most commonly cited reason ABM does not achieve its full potential. If top management does not fully support application of ABM, no one in the organization can own it.

Supportive top management not only includes top management of a company, but also top management of the plant or facility in which ABM is implemented. One company that has been using ABM since the mid-1980s has implemented ABM in only 60 percent of its plants, largely because some plant managers did not want to use ABM in their facilities. While they may be aware of ABM, they have not bought in to its benefits exceeding its costs. They may not yet understand its benefits or may be seeking those benefits through other improvement methods.

A lack of management buy-in and ownership usually manifests itself in managers' failure to supply their time, dedicated people, or devote the funding necessary to implement the project. While leaders may be aware of potential benefits, they're not paying a lot of attention to ABM or playing the role of champion.

Management support should be on board before anyone attempts to apply ABM methods. One way to get them on the northbound train is to position ABM's benefits — results like targeted information for process costing and activity analysis and more accurate information about cost objects (products, services, and customers).

Look at the defense industry. Lack of top management support has crippled its ability to implement ABM. While many defense companies have had successful pilots showing the benefits of changing business practices, very few result in permanent ABM systems. Why? Top management already owns a different view of the business, a view that is focused on viewing costs as required by the Cost Accounting Standards Board and government procurement regulations. More than one ABM project has been stopped at the end of the pilot phase because of fear of creating cost and pricing data subject to government disclosure. Top management teams sometimes believe that the government would require cost reductions on contracts for which the ABC cost turns out to be less than the cost using traditional methods and, conversely, would not allow increases on those contracts for which the ABC cost proves to be higher.

While the Defense Contract Audit Agency (DCAA) has encouraged ABC implementations and promised understanding and support, defense contractors are wary. Many have shifted their focus away from ABC for product costing (and its inherent DCAA risks) to activity analysis. In this shift, the goal is to reduce overall overhead costs. These cost reductions appear to be much more appealing to top management.

Pitfall #2: "Okay, tell me again why we're doing this."

An effective process begins with objectives to which everyone agrees. This is, incidentally, of great help in positioning ABM to top management in the first place. Setting mutually-agreed-upon objectives establishes awareness as well as drives the process.

Without objectives that expose the very definitions of ABM elements, the scope of the method won't get understood, much less implemented. Many people in the awareness stage misunderstand ABC terms such as "cost driver," "cost object," and even the word "activity." Many people mistakenly believe that using ABC information for product costing and for activity analysis are the same thing. In searching to understand what ABM is, the focus shifts (often aided by "experts" selling products) to the specific features of various approaches. These features could be taken from packaged software, a consulting firm's methodology, an article, or a book. In any event, what is lost is the clear purpose of ABM.

For example, the controller of a petrochemical plant on the Gulf Coast was reviewing three proposals to assist his implementation of ABC. He stated that he liked Arthur Andersen's approach to the project but wondered why Arthur Andersen representatives had not brought along a software program to demonstrate. In response, the Arthur Andersen representative offered to demonstrate three off-the-shelf ABC packages, as well as two custom-developed packages. But first he wanted to clarify if the controller was interested in buying software or addressing a business problem. The controller thought for a moment, refocused on his business objective, declined the software reviews, and recommended Arthur Andersen to help solve the business issue. He did the right thing by refocusing on the company's business objective.

Similarly, a manufacturer in the Pacific Northwest requested assistance conducting an ABM pilot in one of its development operations. When asked about the business objective, the company's pilot team stated that they were doing the project because it was in their individual Management by Objectives (MBO) memo for the year. Unfortunately, the engineering group running the development operation did not have it in its MBO, so the pilot did not happen. Why? There was no link to a clear business objective.

Ask the Five Whys

If there is a question about whether an ABM initiative has a clear business objective, the planning team should articulate *why* it is doing the project. Then ask why four more times:[2]

Why is this project being performed?

Because it will make us a better company.

Why will it make us a better company?

Because we will better understand product costs.

Why do you need to understand product costs?

Because we do not understand what causes costs.

Why do we need to understand what causes costs?

Because we have to understand how we can reduce and avoid costs.

Why is reducing and avoiding costs important?

To meet our strategic objective of being the low cost provider.

Answering "why" five times yields the objectives — or demonstrates that the project should not go forward. Get everyone to agree on the objectives, and the initiative is ready for launch.

Pitfall #3: "What do you mean, there are three views of cost?"

Cost management systems can serve at least three distinct purposes: financial, operational, and strategic.[3] These three views include different users, purposes, levels of aggregation, reporting frequency, and types of measures (see Exhibit 1–3). The simple truth is that it's very difficult for a single system, even an activity-based one, simultaneously to meet the requirements of all three of these different views.

The hype over ABC and ABM asserts that ABM can satisfy all internal customers if the method is tailored into a custom process for the company at hand. It begins, though, with understanding and articulating the kinds of financial, operational, and strategic information the company expects. Then the process can be designed to reveal the information in an appropriate sequence.

For example, some companies attempt to develop an ABM system that fulfills strategic product costing and financial reporting purposes at the same time. Strategic product costs normally include costs that are not product costs under Generally Accepted Accounting Principles (GAAP), such as selling and administrative costs. Also, strategic product costs may not include some factory overhead costs (e.g., plant security and plant manager's salary) because they cannot be accurately assigned to individual products. Moreover, strategic product costing may defer costs to future periods such as research and development costs. Likewise, it may currently recognize costs that will be incurred in the future. For

Exhibit 1–3 Three Views of Costs

VIEW	FINANCIAL	OPERATIONAL	STRATEGIC
TIME FOCUS	YESTERDAY	TODAY	TOMORROW
Users of Information	Financial Controllers Tax Managers External Shareholders Lenders Tax Authorities	Line Managers Process Improvement Teams Quality Teams	Strategic Planners Cost Engineers Capital Budgeters Product Sourcing Product Managers
Purposes	Financial Accounting Inventory Valuation Budgeting	Key Performance Indicators (KPIs) Value-/Non-value-Added Indicators Activity Analysis for Process Improvement	Activity-Based Costing Target Costing Investment Justification Life-Cycle Costing Make versus Buy Analysis
Level of Aggregation	High Aggregation Often Companywide Data	Very Detailed Little Aggregation	Plant or Product Line Aggregation What Is Needed for Specific Decision
Reporting Frequency	Periodic, Usually Monthly Probably Could be Quarterly or Annually	Immediate Sometimes Hourly or Daily	Ad Hoc, as Needed Usually a One-Time Study
Type of Measures Needed	Financial	Physical	Both Physical and Financial

Source: This concept was originally developed by Steven Hronec, Arthur Andersen LLP, for an internal training course entitled, "Cost Accounting in the Reinvented Factory of the Future," presented in December 1983. It was first used in this form by Steve Player on an engagement for NordicTrack, October 1993.

example, environmental costs may be estimated and included in strategic product costing for the current year, even though GAAP would not recognize these costs until future years. Consequently, strategic product costs may not be close to GAAP costs.

Therefore, strategic product costs will have to undergo a major revision at the end of the period before they can be used for financial reporting. To avoid this revision, some companies follow GAAP rules when they calculate costs to be used for strategic purposes. The result is costs that are not as relevant as they should be.

Companies can attempt to implement systems intended to present multiple views of costs. Yet there will be trade-offs. The conflicting roles and reasoning behind each view's purpose, users, time focus, and types of measures can compromise a big-picture view. These trade-offs can be mitigated by showing multiple presentation (i.e. both a GAAP view and a strategic life cycle view). However, this multiple-view approach means a geometrically more complex system requirement due to the widely varying levels of aggregation and reporting frequency.

To minimize both compromise and complexity, we recommend that legacy systems feed a common data repository (or warehouse) as noted in Exhibit 1-4. This exhibit illustrates how a company can build a modular system supporting multiple user needs. It reduces cutoff issues by using common data sources while allowing the flexibility of customized user workbenches which focus on each required view of cost. The detail provided for the operational view of costs (operations analysis) can be tailored and changed as the focus of that view moves.

Pitfall #4: "Let's put the controller in charge."

A financial person should not head an ABM project, nor should the ABM team be comprised only of financial people. Otherwise, the project is likely to be viewed as an accounting project. While number crunching is necessary in ABC, ABC numbers must accurately model the organization and must be used for decision making. If both of these conditions are satisfied, an ABC system is transformed into an ABM system.

Putting someone from marketing, operations, or engineering in charge of the project will help ensure that activities and costs are viewed horizontally. Instead of being perceived as an accounting project, ABM will thus be perceived as a management tool that is required for management decision making. This ensures that key linkages of business processes receive visibility, which is often the most insight-awarding benefit of the project.

Exhibit 1–4 Illustrating the Overall Analytical Reporting Vision

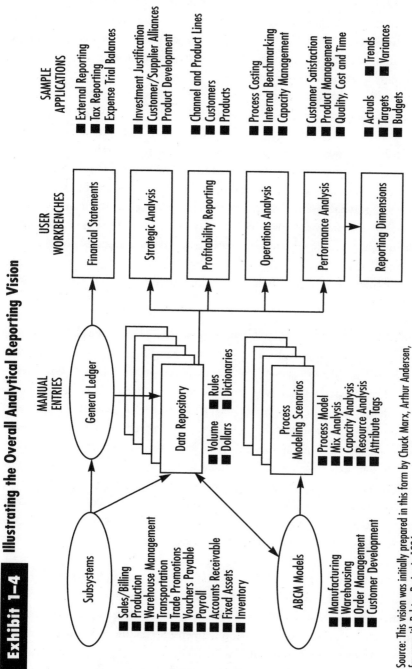

Source: This vision was initially prepared in this form by Chuck Marx, Arthur Andersen, for use with Ralston Purina in 1994.

In a recent review of a Midwest manufacturer, Arthur Andersen consultants analyzed the manufacturer's cost management practices. During the review, the consultants identified five separate cost management systems (financial, purchased material, plant 1 operating, plant 2 operating, and quality cost) in use. This information came as quite a revelation to cost accounting department staff, who only knew about their own system.

Had an ABM project been implemented using only financial personnel, four existing, nonaccounting systems would have been overlooked. A more critical issue, however, is the fact that the needs of those users would not have been understood or addressed. These additional systems often exist because users have acted to meet their own information needs. If additional, nonaccounting systems are present, there is an opportunity to eliminate redundant tasks by implementing an ABM system that includes information supporting them while making it different from the cost accounting system it replaces. This is particularly true in companies in which the traditional cost accounting system focuses on financial accounting, on accountants rather than accounting's customers, and on past information rather than estimated future information. The ABM system must overcome these prior limitations.

Pitfall #5: "We'll tell the employees about this later—maybe."

Employees must be involved in creating, implementing, and continuously improving the ABM system. The identification of activities and cost drivers should be undertaken mainly by nonaccountants. Accountants or outside consultants may facilitate this process, but the identification of activities and related cost drivers must be done by those most knowledgeable about the work: those who do it. Accountants are not experts in knowing what work people are doing, nor are they experts in knowing what causes the work.

Moreover, if nonaccountants are more active in creating the ABM system, they are more likely to use the ABM information and to make suggestions for improving the ABM system. Nonaccountants can spot errors and suggest changes to ensure that the ABM system accurately models operations and tracks operational behavior.

ABM should be viewed as a continuous process in which improvements are normal rather than exceptional. Moreover, ABM must evolve to accurately model organizational changes over time. If ABM is viewed as a one-shot project, any benefits received may be temporal. To ensure that the ABM model evolves, the following steps are essential:

- Integrate activity analysis with the annual planning cycle.

- Link departmental performance measures with departmental activities.
- Include an evaluation of specific critical activities in employee performance appraisals.
- And—most important—tell the employees.

Pitfall #6: "We can do this without spending any money."

A successful ABM system can mean a significant dollar, time and energy investment. Money is often required for ABM expertise either in the form of outside consultants or new permanent employees. Someone must be responsible for leading and managing ABM.

Failure to recognize this is a significant pitfall. For example, one Midwestern manufacturer concluded that due to demands on existing personnel, it would approach the ABM implementation with a part-time project team. To date, it has spent more than a year preparing to launch its ABM effort. In reviewing the cost-to-date (which is still growing), it appears that a dedicated 60-day effort would have been less expensive.

Software is another money issue. Whether packaged software is purchased or a custom system is developed, costs for ABM software can be substantial. Typical projects costs range from a low of $50,000 up to more than $1 million. Packaged software typically runs from $2,500 to $10,000 per site with discounts for multiple site licenses.

Project duration starts at 6–16 weeks for pilot projects. The majority of the implementation stories listed in Section II began with pilots of this duration.

A company that believes an ABM system will provide information that leads to making better decisions should estimate the *value* of those better decisions. This is critical to getting the resources needed to move forward on a rapid and focused basis.

While financial support is necessary, a company must also avoid falling prey to the "big bang" syndrome. That's when a company realizes that the right ABM system can yield tremendous benefits. They get so excited that they agree to spend $10 to $15 million on ABM.

At that investment level, the development effort takes on a life of its own. Consultants are brought in to develop various parts of the system. Software vendors vie to get included in the design. Users lobby to ensure that their needs are addressed. Ultimately more personnel may be brought in simply to manage the complexity of project management.

The risk of the "big bang" approach is that it is often more "noise" than "results." Many things can happen during a two-year development cycle — users change, business needs change, funding priorities may shift. All of these can minimize the impact of any system, no matter how much it costs. An ABM system can easily provide the information needed to save $10 million to $20 million per year—the key is to start saving while you are making the investment.

To achieve this, we recommend a step approach. Take a step toward your long-term direction, but take one that pays an immediate return. The faster your paybacks, the faster you can take your next steps. Our clients often find that this incremental step approach results in a better used system that has more broad-based support, which is critical to a sustained level of funding.

Pitfall #7: "We don't need training—this isn't brain surgery."

ABM may not be brain surgery, but it requires new ways of thinking and adjustments to established routines. People need training.

Usually, initial training is led by outside experts. They can lead subsequent training as well, but the right internal people will do just fine. While internal training may not be as efficient as outside training, company trainers know more about the company and can integrate this knowledge into their training methods.

Both the ABM implementation team and the people using ABM information need to be trained. Much of the training should be done early in the implementation process; however, some training needs to take place after implementation. In addition to training in the general concepts used under ABM, some managers will need specialized training. For example, design engineers should be trained in how to use the ABM system to cost new products.

While this training does require a significant expenditure, ABM may be easier to understand than the old cost system. One company found that an advantage of ABM was that the ABM system was easier to understand. While the old cost system used only one overhead base, and the ABM system ten, the old cost system did not accurately model the factory. Top management wanted its managers to understand the cost system so that better decisions could be made. This goal was easier to achieve under ABM. The company managers had never been able to fully understand the old cost system.

After the initial burst of activity, a periodic follow-up should be conducted to see if this training was effective. This can be ascertained by asking some basic questions:

● Are managers using the ABM system the way it was intended?
● Are managers using activity information as well as product information?
● What difficulties are managers and accountants encountering?

- Do managers understand the ABM information?
- Are there mistakes in the ABM system?
- How can the system be improved?

Training has another benefit. ABM may be outside the comfort zone of many nonaccountants. These people may feel threatened by financial information. Extensive training in ABM helps by allowing them to see how the activities and related costs are determined.

Pitfall #8: "It's the consultant's fault."

Steven M. Hronec, the author of *Vital Signs*, says that there are three reasons to hire a consultant: You don't have the time to do it yourself, you don't know how to do it yourself, or you want someone to blame when things go wrong. The third scenario is no good for anyone, and there are ways to prevent it.

The first warning flag is if a consultant is dictating answers rather than soliciting them. Some consultants try to apply answers found in previous projects rather than finding answers that are appropriate in the current circumstances. A consultant's role is to help the company be successful, a role that includes a healthy dose of knowledge transfer.

The second flag is an ABM model that reflects something other than the stated objectives. An ABM system reflecting the consultant's perception of management's goals and the consultant's perception of the organization may not be effective. The consultants should facilitate management taking ownership of the ABM system—not set a new agenda.

Another variation on this pitfall is purchasing ABC software to "lead you through an implementation." Under this variation, the software takes the role of consultant as "someone to blame when things go wrong." While you may have your scapegoat, you still have failed to meet your business objective.

ABM is not a can of beans that you walk into a store and buy off the shelf. ABM is not prepackaged software that can be spoon-fed to achieve successful results. Software, like consultants, are only tools to facilitate a successful ABM application.

Pitfall #9: "We don't need resident experts."

As recommended under Pitfall #6, at least one person who works permanently at the organization should be an ABM expert. This knowledge may be self-taught, but generally requires collaboration with others. The person may have implemented ABM for another company, may have served as an ABM consultant, or could take the time and make the effort to develop the necessary skills. Someone needs to be permanently responsible for the functional and technical aspects of the ABM system. Not having this expertise will lead to a great deal of frustration and to many missteps.

For example, the finance organization of a coal company sought to use ABM to streamline its accounting activities. For two weeks, each of the 20 employees kept detailed time logs in 15-minute increments, resulting in a pile of useless data. Why is the data useless? The company lacked experience in performing ABM analysis. It failed to establish and use a common activity dictionary and numbering scheme before data collection. Without this step, the activity logs could not be summarized or compared. Employees performing the same tasks would describe them differently. In the end, making sense of the data was impossible, so the project was scrapped.

Initially, cost management expertise can be acquired in the form of outside consultants, work groups, or participation in research groups such as CAM–I. However, when the outsiders leave, someone at the company needs to have this expertise. Knowledge transfer should be required in all projects.

This expertise requirement applies to each operating unit as well as to each company. Someone at each location should be able to understand and operate the system. One company that adopted ABM does not plan to put ABM in all of its operating units because some of those units do not have the necessary cost management expertise.

Pitfall #10: "This doesn't link to other initiatives."

Most companies that implement ABM are also adopting other initiatives such as Just-in-Time (JIT), total quality management (TQM), and business process reengineering (BPR). Rather than implementing ABM in isolation, ABM should be linked with each of these initiatives. ABM provides valuable cost information for JIT, TQM, and BPR decisions. For example, ABM may support BPR by showing that each standard part, rather than a new part, used in a product design will save $1,000. This cost information can be used to encourage actions that are consistent with JIT, TQM, and BPR objectives. Even if ABM cost information indicates that a decision to achieve these objectives will be costly, this is still valuable information. All of these approaches are cost sensitive. For example, actions to improve response time or quality should be taken only if the benefit to the customer exceeds the cost.

Recently, an aircraft manufacturer had a face-off of improvement efforts. The company simultaneously conducted an ABC project, an engineering project, and a theory of constraints project. The goal was to see which one worked best. A better approach would have been to perform all three projects together. Having improvement efforts work together instead of competing is analogous to using multiple horses to pull a wagon. The wagon will travel farther and faster if the horses are pulling in the same direction.

One success story is the ABM implementation at Johnson & Johnson Medical, Inc.[4] Successful ABM pilots caught the eye of TQM process champions who saw it as a better way to measure quality improvements. These TQM process champions became ABM champions as well; eventually, the project team became part of the TQM group. This linkage was the critical factor in the success of ABM at Johnson & Johnson Medical. The project team also used the storyboard techniques of process mapping for both TQM and ABM initiatives (see Chapter 6 for further details).

SOLUTIONS

Getting ABM off the ground is more than possible — it's probable. Especially when these solutions are applied.

Pitfall #1: We can't get the top guys to buy it."

Symptoms

- Lack of enthusiasm or encouragement from top management.
- Difficulty in getting approval for necessary resources such as full-time team members, funding for equipment, or outside resources.
- Failure of management to spend time understanding the initiative or failure to attend briefings.

Treatment

- Link the initiative to key business objectives. Clearly articulate how you will deliver improvement in that area.
- Find an executive who owns the initiative, who will hold an umbrella over it, help it to develop, and showcase the benefits of using ABM. Then use the benefits to convince more people to buy in and own the approach. If successful, this creates a groundswell of support that overwhelms ABM opponents.
- Expose top management to potential benefit of ABM through visits to other successful companies and via benchmarking reports and anecdotes.
- Find competitors who are using or experimenting with the approaches; competition often spurs management into action.

Pitfall #2: "Okay, tell me again why we're doing this."

Symptoms

- Confusion among project team members or management as to the benefits expected from ABM.
- Belief that ABM will simultaneously provide strategic product costing and operational cost reduction output.
- Inability to articulate what will be achieved.
- Confusion over how ABM links to key strategic goals.

Treatment

- Ask management and project teams the "five whys" to focus on the project objective.
- Put the project objectives on paper, circulate them, and review them until consensus is reached. Include how the initiative will deliver on key objectives. State the quantifiable benefits that will be achieved.
- Explicitly state how the project objectives relate to and support key strategic goals.
- Identify any inherent conflicts in objectives (e.g., the design of an ABM system for strategic product costing will create dysfunctional behavior if also used for operational cost reductions).

Pitfall #3: "What do you mean, there are three views of cost?"

Symptoms

- Belief by management that one cost system is meeting everyone's needs.
- Belief that the monthly financial statements are what everyone needs to manage the business.
- Lack of understanding of the role of nonfinancial (physical) performance measures.
- Desire to have an ABM system that efficiently does both product costing and process improvement simultaneously (they seldom do, no matter what the consultant said).
- Belief that traditional variance explanations are still the most efficient way to explain operations.

Treatment

- Search out and identify the other cost systems currently being operated. Identify who uses them, why they exist, and the benefits they provide.
- Track the amount of time spent on special projects because the financial statements did not provide adequate information.

- Educate managers on the use of both physical and financial performance measures.
- Conduct this exercise: Give management financial statements from the last four quarters. Ask them to describe what has happened to customer satisfaction, quality, and on-time delivery over that period. Require them to show their supporting analysis.
- Document the mental steps required to explain traditional variances then show all the steps eliminated if physical measures are used.

Pitfall #4: "Let's put the controller in charge."

Symptoms

- A finance person is chosen to lead the initiative.
- Sales, marketing, and operations personnel exhibit no interest.
- Plan fails to address operational or strategic issues.
- Team struggles with understanding horizontal linkages of processes.

Treatment

- Select a project leader from operations, engineering, marketing, or some other functional area.
- Nonfinancial people should comprise the majority of the team.
- Survey personnel in operations, engineering, and marketing as to what they need. Record their responses, incorporate them, and get their concurrence on the plan.
- Ensure that the initiative links with and supports key business initiatives.
- Use financial people to explain how the tools work. Use operations people to apply the tools to business problems.

Pitfall #5: "We'll tell the employees about this later — maybe."

Symptoms

- Employees are unaware of pilot development efforts.
- Employees are aware of but don't support the effort.
- Survey and data requests go unanswered.
- Review meetings are poorly attended.
- Employees resist using the pilot systems.
- Team is criticized for not understanding the business.

Treatment

- Explicitly link the objectives to achievement of key business goals.
- Select employees for the project team who will operate the system.

- Use "rifle group" meetings instead of surveys to gather data. This involves bringing the people to be interviewed together at the same time.
- Set specific measurable targets for deadlines and hold people accountable for delivery.
- Projects should have focused time frames. Some key goals should be reached in three months or less.

Pitfall #6: "We can do this without spending any money."

Symptoms
- Top management is reluctant to fund the project.
- Manpower, space, and equipment are difficult to acquire.
- Expansion efforts receive lukewarm support.
- Company attempts to use only part-time resources, thus dramatically lengthening the time frame.

Treatment
- Link initiative to key business objectives.
- Articulate a written cost/benefit statement that calculates the cost of permanently lost earnings from not moving forward (savings opportunities foregone).
- If payback is positive, outsource parts of the project or other duties to free up project resources.
- Seek to determine why management is lukewarm and whether their concerns can be addressed.
- Be creative in finding quick hits, low-cost ways to improve (e.g., use off-the-shelf software, cram session pilots, and sample cases).
- Identify a self-funding approach whereby project savings fund further development.

Pitfall #7: "We don't need training—this isn't brain surgery."

Symptoms
- Team is unclear about members' roles or tests that need to be performed.
- Management does not understand how work will change as a result of the new system.
- Frustration is evident; people don't understand the terminology.
- People resist (either passively or actively) using the new approaches because they are unsure of the effect on their jobs.

Treatment

- Conduct orientation training for all who are reluctant to use the new approach. Communicate the business issues being addressed and how the techniques will deal with them.
- Document existing approaches and how they are changing.
- Do a force-field analysis comparing what factors will influence successful implementation (this involves identifying both the forces that are driving and resisting successful implementation).
- Videotape the orientation and training sessions to create on-demand training for new employees and refresher courses.
- Communicate, communicate, communicate (e.g., explain objectives and project status in articles in company newsletters, on a display board, and in a voice-mail hot line).

Pitfall #8: "It's the consultant's fault."

Symptoms

- Initiative belongs to the consultant: "Joe Consultant's Cost System."
- Consultants prescribe rather than describe solutions.
- Company is forced to fit the consultant's model of ABM rather than ABM fitting the company.
- The software, not the company needs, drives the initiative.

Treatment

- Place company people on the project full-time. Insist on full knowledge transfer; by the end of the project, project team members will be as knowledgeable as the consultants.
- Ensure the consultant's attitude is supportive, not dictatorial. The consultant should be offering tools that tie the initiative's success to teamwork with employees and executives.
- Pick an appropriate name and communicate it. Strategic Activity Management (SAM) was Hewlett-Packard–North American Distribution Organization's choice.
- Use consultants as facilitators so that company employees can implement ABM themselves.
- Consultants should be flexible enough to model what company personnel want rather than what the consultants did on their last project.

Pitfall #9: "We don't need resident experts."

Symptoms
- Cost accountants display little understanding of business operations and cost management techniques.
- No cost accounting is being done—there is no cost accounting system, no cost accountants.
- Cost management issues are not understood. There is an inability to answer management questions.
- People are lost as to where to begin or what process to use.

Treatment
- Run the company through a cost management diagnostic to understand key issues. For example, Arthur Andersen's Cost Management Diagnostic shows the relative importance of various costs such as material, labor, and overhead, the relative importance of key components of costs such as payroll, facilities, communications, etc., and the degree of product diversity.
- Select and train a traditional cost accountant or a financial accountant to become a cost management expert.
- Hire in cost management expertise.
- Have consultants train company personnel. Start projects with broad training of ABM and how it will be applied.
- Benchmark cost management practices against global best practices. Understand the differences. For example, Arthur Andersen's Global Best Practices Knowledge Base[SM 5] allows a company to compare its target costing practices to Toyota's, which is considered to be the best in the world.
- Start a cost management library.

Pitfall #10: "This doesn't link to other initiatives."

Symptoms
- The initiative is isolated from other efforts.
- ABM is viewed as a one-time project.
- Product champions of JIT, TQM, BPR, etc., see ABM as a threat (or as unimportant), rather than a resource.

Treatment
- Use ABM to develop performance measurements for JIT or TQM.
- Use ABM to generate ideas for continuous improvement in JIT, TQM, and ABM itself.

- Compare ABM objectives and expected benefits with those of other improvement efforts to identify commonality.
- Include people from other improvement efforts on the ABM steering committee.

Notes

1. Steven M. Hronec, *Vital Signs: Using Quality, Time, and Cost Performance Measures to Chart Your Company's Future* (New York: American Management Association, 1993), 57–61. ABO Continuum is a service mark of Arthur Andersen.

2. See also Mark C. DeLuzio, "The Tools of Just-in-Time," *Journal of Cost Management* (Summer 1993), 19–20.

3. This concept was originally developed by Steven Hronec, Arthur Andersen LLP, for an internal training course. It is touched on briefly in H. Thomas Johnson and Robert S. Kaplan, *Relevance Lost: The Rise and Fall of Management Accounting,* (Boston, MA: Harvard Business School Press), 28 and Robert S. Kaplan, "One Cost System Isn't Enough," *Harvard Business Review* (Jan.–Feb. 1988), 61–66. It is further discussed in Steven M. Hronec, *Vital Signs: Using Quality, Time, and Cost Performance Measures to Chart Your Company's Future* (New York: American Management Association, 1993), 44–45; 130–134.

4. Mark Moelling, "Implementing ABM Under the Umbrella of TQM at Johnson & Johnson," presentation to CAM–I Quarterly Meeting, San Diego, CA, Mar. 1993.

5. The Global Best Practice Knowledge Base[SM] was developed by Arthur Andersen. This information is catalogued on CD-ROM, classified by process.

2

DEVELOPING
THE PILOT

STEVE PLAYER AND DAVID E. KEYS

Hewlett-Packard called Arthur Andersen to draw up a proposal for implementing a strategic activity management system across its North American Distribution Organization. Funding had been approved. Management was committed and ready to start. A talented and dedicated project team was waiting eagerly in the wings.

Due to the need to feed information into the impending planning cycle, the company wanted to go straight to full division implementation—without a pilot. After many warnings, the team remained resolute, so our implementation team charged forward.

Projects like this are truly similar to a battlefield—the conviction and character of your team is tested. Work days stretched to 16 hours, and weekend work became the norm. The group advanced more on faith and fortitude than on favorable results.

The ultimate results of the Hewlett-Packard team's efforts are detailed in Chapter 4. A key lesson out of this story is that there are tremendous benefits to running a pilot. It can be as comprehensive as a full pilot or as simple as piloting a single step, such as how to collect a piece of driver data such as shipments by customer. In either case, developing the pilot can avoid a lot of pain.

To further aid your selection of a successful pilot, we refer you to Appendix II, "Criteria for Selecting Successful Pilot Sites." This checklist was developed by Chuck Marx and Mike Retrum for use by an aerospace manufacturer. It can easily be modified for most companies.

While the pitfalls encountered in getting ABM initiated tend to be behavioral (as are the pitfalls encountered when moving from pilot to mainstream, which are covered in the next chapter), many of the pitfalls that are typically encountered in this phase—developing the pilot ABM system (see Exhibit 2–1)—are technical in nature. They are related to the "nuts and bolts" decisions that have to be made while designing the pilot. Although these pitfalls can cause serious problems in the implementation of ABM, once they are fully understood, they tend to be easier to solve than the behavioral issues.

Exhibit 2-1

Pitfalls in Developing the Pilot

Pitfall #11	"Pilot? We don't need a pilot."
Pitfall #12	"This thing needs a lot of detail."
Pitfall #13	"This thing doesn't need detail."
Pitfall #14	"What are you calling an activity?"
Pitfall #15	"That activity can't cost that much."
Pitfall #16	"We don't keep data that way."
Pitfall #17	"I think we spent that back in '62."
Pitfall #18	"Who picked this software anyway?"
Pitfall #19	"Who needs project management?"
Pitfall #20	"I never dreamed it would take this long."

Pitfall #11: "Pilot? We don't need a pilot."

It is extremely difficult and time-consuming to implement a comprehensive ABM system without doing a pilot first. A large food-processing company in the South decided to implement ABM in one division without doing a smaller pilot first. The division had three large plants in three different states. The company took more than five years to get the ABM system on-line and operating. Using pilots should have dramatically reduced that time.

Doing a pilot first has three advantages. First, the pilot can be structured to increase the chances of its success so that ABM will gain greater support. An area of the company can be selected that has, as it were, ripe, low-hanging fruit.

Second, the effect of mistakes is limited to a single part of the company rather than the whole. Consequently, mistakes can be more easily corrected. A pilot is a learning ground on which improvements in the process are an expected outcome. Third, pilots can be completed in a short period of time. Therefore, feedback on successes and mistakes can be obtained more quickly. This feedback will allow for quicker adjustments to the ABM system and these adjustments will be easier to make.

As noted above, Hewlett-Packard recently implemented a strategic activity management (SAM) model in its North American Distribution Organization. Due to time constraints and the need to coordinate with the existing planning cycle, the decision was made to implement all units without an initial pilot.

Even though the team had deep financial skills and training on project tasks, the team found actual implementation to be very difficult. Through sheer will, long hours, and perseverance, the team was able to complete the implementation. However, the team agreed that a small pilot would have saved time and made full implementation easier to accomplish. (See Chapter 4 for further details.)

Pitfall #12: "This thing needs a lot of detail."

Perhaps the most common technical issue that sinks ABM projects is too much detail. Companies are littered with the wreckage of ABM projects abandoned because the level of detail they attempted to capture was overwhelming. A Gulf Coast food processor, for example, saw its ABM initiative hit the rocks when its PC-based computer systems ran for 12 hours (overnight) to provide updated output. When the project teams found this out, they became discouraged and responded by leaving the ABM initiative behind (along with their hopes of what ABM was supposed to do for them).

At user group meetings for commercial software packages that specialize in ABM, a key discussion item is how to get more out of these systems. New entrants into the field often tout the speed of their new software compared to the market leaders. While their claims must be carefully evaluated to understand the real performance issues, the more central question lies in understanding how much detail is truly needed. Without such an understanding it is easy to envision systems that would have difficulty running on large mainframe systems, much less on a PC.

Activity-based systems often capture the imagination of operating and financial personnel who have longed for the ability to view cost in multiple dimensions rather than in the typical single dimension of traditional systems. Teams want ABC to include product costing with detailed activity levels, customer costing, and distribution channel costing. The teams want ABM to include process costing, value-added analysis, and cost of quality. Excitement grows as teams visualize the ability to view costs by the degree to which they vary; not just the variable, semivariable, and fixed classifications, but also the ability to describe costs as unit-level, batch-level, product-level, process-sustaining, facility-sustaining, customer-sustaining, or entity-required.

The visualization process can get to be overwhelming as teams dream of producing these reports at the push of a PC button: hit F12 and out the reports come. All of the items noted above can be included in ABM; however, it is difficult, to do them simultaneously.

It also is extremely expensive in terms of maintenance costs. Each bit of activity information has to be identified, collected, and costed. Driver information has to be identified, collected, and related to its usage by cost objects. Treatment of items unrelated to the cost objects have to be discussed and resolved. Is all of this effort worth it? That depends on the value of decisions a company makes as a result of the data.

Exhibit 2–2 graphically depicts the relationship of the cost of data collection with the percentage of potentially relevant data collected. It demonstrates that if the amount of data is kept to a minimum, and the data is relevant, the cost of data collection can be kept quite low. It is a premise applicable to strategic cost systems, in which not as much detailed information is needed as is required in an operational cost system (discussed in Chapter 1, Pitfall #3).

Exhibit 2–2 also demonstrates the effect on cost of data collection as the percentage of potentially relevant data collected approaches 100 percent. As the level of detail increases in order to achieve higher levels of relevance, cost of data collection skyrockets, a logical occurrence because data that is easier to collect will be collected first. For example, the first activity driver in the ABM system may provide 20 percent of the potentially relevant data. The fifteenth driver in the ABM system may only provide two percent of the potentially relevant data.

How much relevance is worthwhile? The value of improved decision making as a result of increasing relevance and detail needs to be compared to the cost of more data (including data collection costs).

Pitfall #13: "This thing doesn't need detail."

Too little detail is as bad as too much detail. Too little detail generally results from two different misuses of ABC. The first is the assertion or belief that an activity-based system has been implemented when, in fact, it has not, an error usually born of the general confusion that surrounded many early discussions about ABC. Companies implemented detailed versions of their traditional cost systems using multiple pools and multiple drivers. However, the fundamental step of defining work on an activity basis was never taken.

These multipool, multidriver systems are often mistaken for ABC systems. And, although in many cases they are dramatic improvements over preexisting single driver systems, unfortunately, they typically provide too little detail to yield an understanding of what work really goes on in a company.

The second misuse usually occurs when companies attempt operational improvement, such as cost reduction, with an ABM model designed for strategic purposes. The conflict in these views of costs (see Chapter 1, Pitfall #3 and Exhibit 1–3) often results in operating managers shifting their focus to manage

Exhibit 2-2

The Relationship of Cost of Data Collection to the Percentage of Potentially Relevant Data Collected

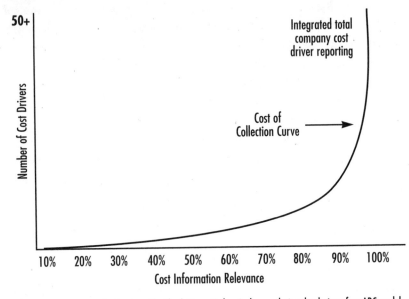

Source: This concept was originally developed by Chuck Marx, Arthur Andersen, during the design of an ABC model at FMC Corporation in 1989.

output measures (used by the strategic view to assign costs) instead of managing the underlying activities.[1]

The root cause of misunderstanding often lies in confusion over the term "cost driver." The industry-accepted definition of a cost driver is: "any factor that causes a change in the cost of an activity."[2] However, the term is often used incorrectly to describe the output of an activity. The output of an activity should be referred to as an activity driver, "a measure of the frequency and intensity of the demands placed on activities by cost objects.... Sometimes an activity driver is used as an indicator of the output of an activity...."[3]

For strategic purposes, activity drivers, not cost drivers, are used to assign costs; the cost of collecting data for cost drivers would be prohibitively high since there are so many of them. For operational purposes, this detail is necessary to achieving objectives. Cost drivers need to be identified and measured so that the factors that cause costs can be understood.

Take a purchasing process as an example. For strategic purposes such as product costing, the activity costs of purchasing are often assigned to products by an activity driver such as the number of purchase orders for the product. Gathering volume data on the number of purchase orders can usually be done easily, and the purchase orders can be related easily to the products receiving the benefit from them.

But what happens if the manager of the purchasing department tries to use this strategic information for operational purposes? Does it provide the information necessary for the manager to understand what causes cost to occur in purchasing? It does not, because there is too little detail. At best, the information can be used as a targeting tool. At worst, the manager will eliminate purchase orders that should not be eliminated.

From an operational standpoint, the level of detail in information necessary to understand what causes cost to occur in purchasing could include information on:

- number of vendors as well as a breakdown of existing versus new vendors;
- number of vendor audits;
- type of items purchased (commodity versus specialty);
- type of paperwork used;
- type of computer systems used;
- organizational structure of the purchasing department;
- purchasing policies and procedures;
- locations and types of operations supported;
- activities of the purchasing department.

The level of additional detail would continue to expand until its cost exceeded the benefit—in this case, in terms of cost reduction opportunities, of collecting and analyzing it.

A company's success depends not on the number of activities or drivers it uses but on how relevant that number is to a specific business objective. For example, Tektronix has two activities and two drivers in the cost system utilized in its oscilloscope plant.[4] On the other hand, Caterpillar uses multiple cost systems, many cost centers, and several overhead bases.[5] Caterpillar has a separate cost pool for each machine. Both companies are leaders in their respective industries and have been successful in competing against foreign competition.

As a rule of thumb, a strategic costing system with 15 to 50 drivers is generally adequate. Coca-Cola management, in its implementation of ABC in its worldwide manufacturing plants, limited drivers to 35.

For operational purposes, drill down into the detail activities and drivers until an understanding of what causes cost to occur is established. This detail can then be used to restructure or reengineer operations.

At a large Midwestern food processing company, 1,500 activities were identified during a reengineering initiative. During the subsequent implementation of ABM, this list was reduced to 150. For product costing purposes, no more than 45 drivers were used.

After restructuring has occurred, the value of continuing to collect the data is questionable. It's best to stop the collection of cost driver data and instead trace three to six key performance measures for processes. These are monitored until the performance goes out of control or it is again time to focus on improving the area. At that point, the process is repeated.

Pitfall #14: "What are you calling an activity?"

ABM is about activities. Collecting data about them is essential but can be a problem. The best way to start is by addressing the three fundamental problems in collecting activity data:

- To what level should activities be defined?
- What level of data reliability is required?
- What method can be used to efficiently capture this data?

The first fundamental problem in ABC/ABM applications is poor definition of individual activities. People who perform the same tasks describe them in vastly different terms. Often, it seems as if common activities cannot be identified.

How can this pitfall be avoided? First, develop a standard activity dictionary. The dictionary would include a key-word definition of each activity, which would allow identification of common activities performed by various staff members. (Many consulting firms have industry-specific activity dictionaries accumulated from prior experiences; these provide a good starting point, but must be customized for each company.)

The next step is to link activity dictionaries to process mapping documentation and thereby attach costs to the horizontal business processes. Arthur Andersen, in partnership with the International Benchmarking Clearinghouse (IBC), developed a process classification scheme for use in benchmarking processes even though they may cross industry boundaries. The IBC uses this process classification scheme as a universal language for benchmarking research (see Exhibit 2–3).

Arthur Andersen is currently integrating its industry-specific activity dictionaries around the coding structure of the process classification scheme, a linkage that will facilitate benchmarking of activity-based costs as well as process steps. Use of alphanumeric code numbers with activities greatly facilitates rolling up the data.

Exhibit 2-3

Process Classification Scheme

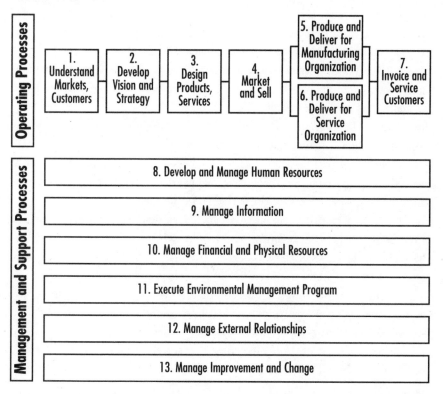

Source: Arthur Andersen's Global Best Practices Knowledge Base and the International Benchmarking Clearinghouse.

The second fundamental problem is the level of reliability of the activity data. This can become a problem depending on the perceived use of the information. Reliability in data collection may suffer from unintentional or intentional bias. When employees are asked about how their time is spent, care must be exercised to insure that the most recent time frame does not taint the perception of the full year. Also, when people are afraid they'll lose their jobs, they may misstate things deliberately in the belief that ABM will result in a new round of cost cutting. Other people may bias data to make favorite products, activities, or functions look like they are performing better than they actually are. Idle time or non-value-added tasks are often omitted or ignored in this scenario. That's why some surveys show widely varying perceptions of the work being done. Nonmanagement personnel may disagree with each other, and sometimes differ with management about the work being done. Such disagreements can be caused by honest differences of opinion as well as deliberate misstatements of information.

Closely related to data reliability is the third fundamental problem with collecting activity data: What method can be used to efficiently capture the data? The two key items to focus on within the methods are (1) the level from which to collect data and (2) the type of data collection method.

The level from which the data is collected ranges from key functional managers down to individual workers. At Southwestern Bell, an activity-based approach was used in reengineering the company's finance and administrative functions. A determination was made to gather and survey all employees in the area (more than 3,000). Management believed that the benefits of having all employees participate in the process would greatly speed implementation of needed changes. Management felt that the benefits of having all employees participate was greater than the cost of the data collection.

Types of data collection methods include individual interviews, surveys, focus groups (e.g., rifle meetings and storyboard sessions), and time studies. **Individual interviews** are a rich source of data but often are too costly for large groups. **Surveys,** one of the older but still widely used forms of data collection, work well in cases in which activity information is being gathered from numerous locations. Surveys can include videos providing standardized instructions and paper-based examples of how to prepare the data.

Focus groups, such as rifle meetings and storyboard sessions, are modified survey approaches. They seek to dramatically reduce the cycle time required to gather the data in the survey approach. In a **rifle meeting,** a standard survey approach is used, but managers provide the data for the survey in the rifle meeting rather than waiting until after the meeting. This approach provides immediate feedback on what information has been provided and what information needs to be obtained. Questions from survey respondents are answered immediately in front of the entire group. This increases the level of understanding in the group and increases the level of consistency of responses.

Storyboarding was first applied to ABM by Mark Moelling at Johnson & Johnson Medical, Inc. (see Chapter 6 for further details). The ABM team sought to identify activities in a rapid visual fashion by mapping the activities of a process. They adopted the visual storyboard approach used by Walt Disney for the development of animated cartoons. The team added brainstorming rules and ice breakers such as stress bags (balloons filled with sand for squeezing) and killer balls (foam balls that are thrown at verbose speakers to tone them down). These techniques have shortened the cycle time while increasing the information developed by these sessions. Moelling has developed a customized version of storyboarding called Rapid Vision^{SM} which is commercially available to project teams.

Time studies, perhaps the oldest method of data collection, can include videotaping, motion analysis, detail reviews, and sampling techniques. They represent a highly accurate method of collecting activity data. Unfortunately, a time study's cost of collection is extremely high, which limits the method's use to very limited areas such as preparing an activity analysis of a machine setup for a setup-reduction study. A detailed time study provides more reliable information than a survey; however, it also costs a lot more.

These data collection methods continue to evolve, especially in light of the development of software programs for electronic polling and collection of activity information. Technology may soon assist in collection of activity data with faster turnaround and on a more cost-effective basis.

A number of Arthur Andersen implementations over the past two years have used Microsoft Access databases to speed the collection and processing of activity data. This approach increases the flexibility of activity information reporting and prepares the data for feeding into an off-the-shelf ABC package.

Pitfall #15: "That activity can't cost that much."

ABM assignments are not intended to be precisely accurate. However, they have to be accurate enough to use for decision making. In fact, one of the main advantages of ABM versus traditional cost systems is that ABM cost assignments are *more* accurate than traditional cost allocations. Even under ABM, however, care must be taken to accurately assign costs to activities and to cost objects. Otherwise, inaccuracies will still exist.

For example, in ABM, managers' salaries are often assigned to activities using estimates of how managers say they spent their time. Often, no records are kept and no observation takes place to verify the estimates. Managers may not be able to accurately remember how they spent their time. Moreover, they may want to bias ABM costs to make some activities (or other cost objects) look more costly and others look less costly.

One company had a CEO who enjoyed the exposure he received from selling to nonprofit organizations such as schools and police organizations. A large percentage of the company's sales were to these nonprofit organizations even though the company's competitors would not even bid on this type of work, which company personnel, including the company's accountant, were sure was unprofitable. The CEO's time estimates for the nonprofit work were suspect.

Using time estimates from his own observations and from other managers' observations that were significantly different than the CEO's, the accountant showed the sales to nonprofit organizations to be unprofitable. The information was used by the company's owner to confront the CEO.

Another example of inaccurate allocation is when revenues are used as a cost driver. ABM cost drivers should have a cause and effect relationship with cost, i.e., the cost driver should be the cause of the cost. Sales may be a cost driver in a few isolated cases such as (1) commission payments based solely on sales, (2) sales taxes, and (3) retail store rents billed as a percentage of sales. However, in most cases where sales are used as a driver, the cause and effect relationship is woefully inadequate. Some prime examples include allocation of insurance costs as flat percentage across all sales rather than based on history, bad debts as a percentage of sales and selling, and general and administrative costs. These arbitrary allocations taint the believability of the ABM system as they fail to reflect cause-and-effect relationships.

For example, one company's consultants allocated one pool of activity cost using revenues as the cost driver. This pool of cost was a miscellaneous aggregation of costs for which the consultants could not find a cause. The company's top management wanted all costs allocated so that they could make sure "all costs were covered." The company's traditional cost system allocated many of these same costs using revenues, which blurred the distinction between the ABM and the traditional system. Managers were skeptical when they were told that the ABM costs were accurate and were the result of cause and effect assignments. If assignments are not reasonably accurate, they should not be made. Making them reinforces the misperception that ABM is a traditional cost system.

Pitfall #16: "We don't keep data that way."

ABM systems are more detailed than traditional systems, a fact that is true not only for the collection of activity data, but also in the detail required to associate these activities to the cost objects. After an activity driver is identified, the project team must gather data on how many units of that driver are consumed by each cost object. In seeking to obtain the data, the response often given is, "We don't keep data that way."

Financially based information systems often fail to track the operational detail needed for cost drivers and activity drivers. Physical measures may exist as part of the operational reporting systems. However, the sheer volume of this data and the need for this information on a timely, rather than historical, basis often results in failure to maintain accurate and detailed historical records.

When the data is captured, it is often only captured at a highly aggregated level, permitting some activity-based analysis but lacking the detail needed for costing on an item-by-item basis. For instance, a project team may be able to determine the total number of shipments made for the year and be able to determine the average cost per shipment. However, it will be unable to complete a customer costing analysis unless it can obtain driver data about the number of shipments made to each individual customer.

In general, companies that have detailed traditional cost systems will have an easier time implementing ABM.[6] A detailed cost system will already include much of the driver information required by the ABM system. One large Midwestern company with a detailed traditional cost system found that nine out of ten of the activity drivers selected for its ABM system were already being collected.

If activity and cost driver information is already being collected, the cost of implementing ABM will be significantly lower than if it is not. When selecting ABM activity and cost drivers, some companies give preference to drivers that are already being gathered or drivers that will be easier to collect.

In situations in which detailed data is not readily available, companies can use surrogate activity drivers, using the number of production runs as a surrogate for material disbursing activities, for example.[7] While the number of material disbursements may not be tracked, the number of production runs generally are. If there is a close relationship between the number of disbursements and each production run (e.g., three disbursements for every production run), then production runs can serve as a surrogate activity driver. Other methods of overcoming the unavailability of data include statistical sampling of transactions and using estimates made by operational personnel.

Pitfall #17: "I think we spent that back in '62."

ABC systems take costs of a given year, trace those costs to activities, and then assign activity costs to business processes, products, services, or customers. ABC systems often use only general ledger costs, which are defined by GAAP. Under GAAP, costs are assigned to a given year based on a historical cost basis. Unfortunately, GAAP rules often do not result in costs being assigned to the right year.[8] The right year is the year in which the cost produces benefit. For strategic purposes, an ABC system gives greater emphasis to the matching principle than GAAP does. GAAP relies more heavily on the principle of conservatism, which causes certain types of costs to be expensed rather than capitalized.

For example, under GAAP, selling, administrative, and research and development salaries are assigned to the year in which the salaries are earned by the employees. No effort is made to assign salaries to the year in which they generate benefit. To the extent that these salaried people benefit future periods, their salaries will be assigned to the wrong year, eliminating the chance that they will be assigned to the correct product or other cost object. The correct cost object is not necessarily in the same year as the expense; it is in the year in which the benefit is generated.

The same is true for depreciation. Useful lives, salvage value, and selection of depreciation method may be based on regulatory rules to effect income for financial accounting or tax purposes. If the same depreciation numbers are used for the ABM system, they may not reflect the true economic consumption of the related assets. We have seen countless instances of low or no depreciation in some plants to artificially high amounts caused by acquisition accounting rules. If depreciation dollars use an incorrect amount or are assigned to the wrong year, there is no chance that they will be properly assigned to the correct cost object.

Proper assignment of costs to the cost object is the basis of life-cycle costing.[9] Unlike GAAP, which expenses costs as they are incurred, the life-cycle approach relates costs to the correct cost object and focuses on nonrecurring costs such as preproduction design and development as well as postproduction support. The life-cycle view is essential to understanding the difference between when costs become committed and when their related cash flow physically occurs. For example, 80 percent of production costs become committed during the design phase but are incurred during production. Exhibit 2–4 illustrates the difference between when costs are committed versus when they are incurred. The life-cycle view is also necessary for relating costs to the corresponding benefits they produce.

Pitfall #18: "Who picked this software anyway?"

Software specifically designed for ABM represents a relatively new but rapidly expanding application area. The first ABC software forum, hosted by CAM–I in May 1990, was attended by eight vendors. Of the products demonstrated, seven were PC-based, one was mainframe-based and focused on the process industry. Three of the products were owned or licensed by consulting firms and were only available with the purchase of their services.

Five years later, all seven of the PC-based products remain available and at least an additional six have been introduced. Mainframe development has been slower, but many vendors discuss packages with ABM functionality such as Oracle, Dun & Bradstreet; SAP; Marcom's Prism; and Andersen Consulting's Process 1. While product introductions have increased, so has the diversity of

Development Influence Over Costs

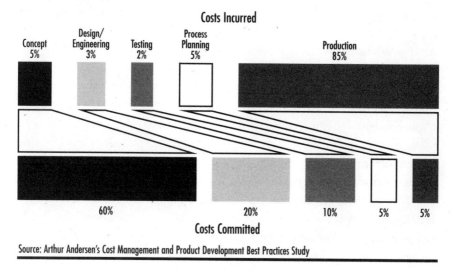

Source: Arthur Andersen's Cost Management and Product Development Best Practices Study

the features they offer, which has continued as more mainframe software vendors and providers of executive information and decision support systems have entered the field. The move to client server and network solutions has added to the diversity as well. All of this activity results in a high degree of variation in the functionality, performance, and cost of each package.[10] And greater challenges.

Six key problems seem to occur in the realm of ABM software tools. Many relate to PC-based software; new versions of the programs attempt to address these issues (although in-depth analysis of the problems of software tools is beyond the scope of this book, a summary of them follows).

First, PC-based systems are often stand-alone units, which can limit access to the results of the project. Lack of user access is cited as a key reason for the failure of many PC-based ABM systems.[11] Since most PC systems have limited capability to support various users, managers who need ABM information may have difficulty accessing it. Some companies use the PC system to deliberately limit access, due to fears of copying and unauthorized access to sensitive cost information. Limited access also limits users' ability to experiment and become more familiar with the ABM system. And, limited access can breed distrust. Managers cannot be expected to be fully supportive of a new system until they can use it and understand the benefits it can provide.

Second, PC-based ABM systems are often constrained by the hardware's own limitations, such as the speed of the central processing unit, data storage capacity, and the speed of input/output devices, all of which limit the level of detail that can be captured. Careful analysis and planning that places emphasis on including the most important data in the ABM system can help circumvent hardware limitations.

For example, several years ago, Arthur Andersen developed an ABM initiative using a Compete model. When loaded with activity data from all employees, the model's performance became intolerable. The model had to be broken into subsets for consolidation. (Note: subsequent versions of Compete are said to provide better use of the math co-processor, thereby enhancing performance when making multiple calculations). When performing both product costing and customer profitability, separation of a model into two pieces will enhance performance, often justifying the added cost of maintaining two models.

Third, as is the case with many new software applications, those specifically designed for ABM have been developed by entrepreneurial companies that do not possess deep financial resources. Consequently, postsale support to learn and understand how the models can be used is generally provided only by the market leaders. In addition, many small software houses do not have the resources to take advantage of recent software developments. Some haven't yet adopted the Windows interface; some who have adopted it merely overlaid it without developing the necessary structures to use it efficiently.

Fourth, from a practical standpoint, importing client data to populate resource accounts, resource drivers, and activity drivers is often difficult to achieve. Users also experience difficulty in printing screens or other documentation to help in model upkeep and maintenance. Poor quality in the reports of results is a major problem. Output data often has to be placed in a more user-friendly spreadsheet or database application for report generation.

Fifth, because ABM packages are custom designed, changes can be very costly. Companies who have rejected off-the-shelf packages often find that custom development is even more costly. The problem is compounded by a lack of understanding of what the ABM system should do. Yet many project teams have found that purchasing an off-the-shelf package facilitates their learning and understanding of what the ABM system should do, which enables the team to adapt more easily if custom development is deemed necessary at a later date.

The sixth problem is perhaps the most deadly. Some companies make the mistake of focusing on the software and what it does, rather than on the decisions to be made with the information it generates.

For example, a particular software package has a function that allows companies to break activities into tasks, providing much more detailed information than is generally required for cost assignment to cost objects (the strategic view of costs). Companies that have used the software feature to simultaneously assign costs to products and get task information are quickly overwhelmed by the data required.

While the computer decreases the computing cost of keeping detailed information, it does not decrease the time required to generate and understand the information. Software vendors attempt to build in as many options as possible, broadening their potential sales base. An effective user is one who knows exactly which features are needed to meet the business objective, and does not make the mistake of trying to use them all.

Pitfall #19: "Who needs project management?"

Any large-scale improvement initiative may not survive poor project management. CAM–I members reported that project management is the key factor in the success of their efforts.

The team leader role is critical. It is important to select someone who understands the business and works well with people from many functional areas within the company. The stature of the person selected to lead will affect the rest of the organization's perception dramatically. But the selected individual's stature should be related to his or her effectiveness in leading teams to reaching objectives; management talent must be the criterion.

The second management aspect is selection of team members who will carry out the tasks, inform and interact with the organization, and be charged with ensuring that the ABM model accurately reflects the operation. Their willingness and desire to participate in the effort coupled with their understanding of the business and the people in it are critical to success.

After the selection of people, the next management element is training. Training sessions should include the team, the steering committee, and ultimately the end users of the system. Experience demonstrates that it is much better to use exercises and case studies to provide practical experiences, rather than lectures focusing on ABM theory.

Solid task management is the fourth element. This includes work plans "illuminated" by examples of actual deliverables. The plan should feature steps or tasks with time and cost budgets and a mechanism for monitoring progress.

Teams often have problems communicating among themselves and with the rest of the organization. As a major change initiative, the ABM process should include a communication plan. Objectives should be stated and comfirmed against the expectations of team members, end users and stakeholders.

A good measure of how an initiative is going can be found in the attendance at team meetings and status meetings. Missed meetings are not a good sign, especially if absentees give no reason or if their excuses appear weak. Poor attendance may signal that the participants are losing faith in the importance of the ABM project, an issue to be addressed immediately. This is best addressed by meeting individually with participants to reconfirm their buy-in and commitment to the initiative. It may be necessary to remind them of the business objective and how ABM will achieve that objective.

Lack of communication can cause several problems including: the project running behind schedule, the project cost exceeding budget, lack of knowledge of project status, and lack of knowledge about how ABM information will be used. To avoid communication gaps, steering committee meeting minutes should be published and posted. Any gaps should be closed up front.

If major milestones are missed, an immediate review should be conducted to determine what went wrong and what can be done to correct the problem. If necessary, cost estimates and due dates should be adjusted as soon as the required changes are known. These changes should be communicated quickly to minimize the potential negative impacts of a surprise.

Pitfall #20: "I never dreamed it would take this long."

Many companies fall into the trap of not giving people enough time to implement ABM. Any pilot will fail when the company does not dedicate the resources necessary for it to succeed. It's like planting seeds but not taking the time to water the plants. Growth may occur, but the crop will never reach its full potential; often, it yields no fruit.

One Fortune 500 company had conducted successive rounds of downsizing, leaving remaining managers under intense pressure to get the work done. It also had implemented ABC pilots at three test sites. Managers were negative about ABC because of the amount of time they had to spend identifying activities and drivers. Afterward, little time was left for analysis or development of procedures by which the data could be used. Ultimately, the pilots were rejected and the company returned to its traditional cost accounting system.

One can only speculate as to what the results would have been had sufficient resources been dedicated to the pilot. Analysis of the activity data may well have identified non-value-added activities that could be reengineered to yield more sustainable results. Typical downsizing often fails to work because elimination of people does not eliminate work. Two years after downsizing, many organizations still retain the same broken processes and problems. Downsizing is like a crash diet—temporary reduction results, but the lasting effects are often negative. Understanding and eliminating activities in order to fundamentally restructure processes, which requires full-time resources, are the only ways to lasting improvement.

When people have been dedicated on a full-time basis to ABM pilots, some remarkable results have occurred. One notable example is at Deere and Company. In 1985, Keith Williams was given two to three months to conceptualize a new cost system.[12] As a result, he came up with the terminology "activity-based costing, cost drivers, and cost buckets" and developed the conceptual model for ABM at Deere.

Solutions

It's easy for accountants who have not implemented ABM successfully to overstate the importance of technical issues. The accountants interviewed in this research project had a better understanding of the technical issues of designing a cost management system than the behavioral issues of using a cost management system for decision making. Before implementing ABM, they tended to overemphasize the technical issues; as ABM was implemented, they tended to emphasize the behavioral issues more.

In contrast, successful users of ABM information emphasized the behavioral issues before, during, and after ABM implementation. They tended to concern themselves with technical issues as they relate to the behavioral issues. For example, if a technical issue affected decision making in a negative manner, then users became concerned. The behavioral issues discussed in Chapter 3 are good examples of these points.

Any one of the technical pitfalls discussed in this chapter can cause an ABM pilot to fail. On the other hand, if the pitfalls are recognized and addressed, the pilot will succeed and the ABM system will have a better chance at long-term survival.

SUMMARY
Pitfall #11: "Pilot? We don't need a pilot."
Symptoms
- Management believes that a pilot is not necessary.
- Complexity of ABM is underestimated.
- Time to complete a comprehensive ABM system is underestimated.
- Advantages of a pilot are minimized.

Treatment
- Describe in detail the specific characteristics and steps required in a comprehensive ABM system and point out that a pilot generates experience and comfort with the concepts.
- Point out the advantages of a pilot and the risks of not doing one.
- If companywide implementation is attempted, train with case-study examples and exercises to give hands-on experience; select small portions of the total engagement that can be completed first (i.e. pilot within the total project).

Pitfall #12: "This thing needs a lot of detail."

Symptoms
- The number of activities for which detailed driver information must be gathered is overwhelming. The cost of collecting the data often outweighs its benefits.
- The PC-based model takes hours to calculate.
- There appear to be no significant activities.
- Individual workers are each performing a multitude of activities.
- The initiative generates a tremendous amount of data but little information showing how activities relate to each other.

Treatment
- Have a clear understanding of why the initiative is being undertaken. What is the business problem it is attempting to solve? Use the understanding to focus on the right level of detail.
- Limit the number of activities to those that are significant (i.e. you must spend five percent or more of your time on it).
- Consolidate into common activities.
- Include information on how activities interrelate instead of detailed data on individual tasks.

Pitfall #13: "This thing doesn't need detail."

Symptoms
- Activities, as defined, bear a strong resemblance to functional department titles.
- People reviewing the activity-based system design can only see a more detailed version of a traditional cost accounting system.
- Activity attributes can not be clearly identified (i.e., an activity is defined at a high level so that a portion is value-added and a portion is non-value-added).
- Activity analysis provides little insight on the existing operational problems.

- Management attempts to reduce operational cost using a model designed for strategic costing purposes.

Treatment

- Make sure that activities are defined rather than functional department names.
- Identify the linkages of activities to form processes. Note how these processes cross horizontal lines.
- Understand the view of cost that the model attempts to address. If shifting from a strategic view to an operational view, realize that drilling down for additional detail is necessary.
- Determine if activities are defined at a level low enough to easily facilitate attribute flagging or tagging.

Pitfall #14: "What are you calling an activity?"

Symptoms

- Level of people interviewed is not perceived to reveal detailed understanding of the work.
- Survey results are tainted by fear that employees may lose their jobs.
- Detailed surveys of individual workers show widely varying perceptions of the work done.
- Management's view of activities being performed is widely different than workers'.
- Collection of activity data is taking too long.

Treatment

- Consider interviewing those doing the work rather than supervisors. (This may be critical if the ABM system is to be used for the operational view of cost.)
- Consider using the storyboarding technique to involve employees in activity definition. Participation helps mitigate fear.
- Verify survey data. Ask more than one person the same question or observe the work being performed.
- Speed collection of activity information by using rifle meetings or the storyboarding technique.

Pitfall #15: "That activity can't cost that much."

Symptoms

- Costs are allocated to cost objects for which there is no cause and effect relationship (true to some degree in almost all cases in which the full costing concept is used within an ABC system).

- Operating managers complain that the output measures used to assign costs do not reflect economic reality.
- Managers complain that cost driver data is inaccurately recorded or out of date.
- Capacity assumptions in the model do not agree with what really happens. It does not match theoretical, practical, normal, budgeted, or actual capacity.

Treatment
- Do not allocate costs if they cannot be assigned reasonably accurately.
- Use cause and effect relationships to establish activity drivers for assignment of costs.
- Make sure that cost drivers are accurately recorded (in determining actual values of cost drivers) and review ABM data every year.
- Use practical capacity to assign costs to cost objects. Review capacity assumptions with operating managers. Compare actual capacity with assumptions to ensure timely updates.

Pitfall #16: "We don't keep data that way."

Symptoms
- Transaction-level detail is not maintained on a regular basis. Summary detail does not permit tracing to cost objects on an item-by-item basis.
- Information systems are financially based. They do not track physical measures.
- Key cost driver data does not appear to be readily available.
- Detail data at the task level (such as number of sales calls by customer or number of receipts by product) is not readily available.

Treatment
- Identify surrogate activity drivers to minimize the number of drivers required and to minimize the cost of data collection.
- Translate operational (nonfinancial) systems to determine the physical measures they track.
- Gradually increase the level of detail of data collected and used.
- Identify where systems can be enhanced to track and summarize drivers by the required detail cost object level.
- Gather data on a sampling basis.

Pitfall #17: "I think we spent that back in '62."

Symptoms

- Costs to be assigned under the ABM system are equal to those under the traditional system (based on the financial view of costs).
- Embedded research and development costs are allocated to existing products instead of future products.
- Costs (such as training, new product development, brand advertising, etc.) benefitting future periods are charged to current periods.
- Life-cycle costing is not used.

Treatment

- Adopt a life-cycle costing approach particularly when using the strategic view of costs.
- Assign salaries to the period that receives the benefit from those salaries.
- Make sure depreciation estimates (method, useful life, and salvage value) are accurate in that they represent economic reality.
- When selecting specific items within a cost object, be sure to include unidentified new products or services as an item to which cost can be traced.

Pitfall #18: "Who picked this software anyway?"

Symptoms

- Importing data into cost models is difficult.
- Report generation is difficult.
- The selected system is PC-based, limiting its size and usefulness while compromising security.
- The selected system was purchased from a relatively new niche firm with limited development resources.
- Custom software changes appear to be cost-prohibitive.
- The team finds itself conforming to software requirements rather than using software to meet company business needs.

Treatment

- Arrange for software demonstrations. View examples of the reports that can be generated. Understand how data can be imported.
- Adapt a commonly used software package. Ask for and check references of industry (or related industry) use.
- Consider customized software only after learning from a standard software package.

- Keep business objectives firmly in mind. Identify and use software features that help meet that objective. Save the rest for when and if objectives change.

Pitfall #19: "Who needs project management?"

Symptoms
- Initiative is over budget.
- Initiative is not delivered on time.
- No one seems informed about the initiative's current status.
- Expected users of the information do not know what the new system will do for them.
- Team members miss team meetings.
- There are surprises.

Treatment
- Select a project team leader who understands the business and works well with people from all functional areas that will be affected.
- Provide extensive training for the project team, steering committee, and expected users of the system. Use exercises and case studies to give them hands-on experience.
- Communicate objectives and record interim results as they occur. Put them in writing and circulate them liberally.
- Keep a running summary of costs as they are committed and incurred. Track weekly burn rate and continually update estimates for project completion.
- Set deadlines for each phase as well as interim steps with specific deliverables.
- If a major milestone is missed, conduct an immediate review to determine what went wrong and what can be done to put things back on track.

Pitfall #20: "I never dreamed it would take this long."

Symptoms
- The company has downsized by arbitrarily terminating people rather than systematically using activity analysis to eliminate work.
- People are not prepared for meetings.
- People miss meetings.
- People are fighting brush fires. The company is in a reactive mode.
- People do not have enough time to devote to project tasks. Excessive amounts of overtime are being logged.

Treatment

- Devote some key employees to the initiative on a full-time basis.
- Hire temporary people to fill in on regular jobs for permanent employees assigned to the project.
- Give ABM a higher priority by focusing on its expected benefits. If competing objectives are present, focus ABM on how it can support the primary objective.
- Use consultants to a greater extent but only in facilitating and support roles.

Notes

1. For further discussion, see "Pitfalls in Using ABC Cost Driver Information to Manage Operating Costs" by H. Thomas Johnson, R. Steven Player, and Thomas P. Vance, *Corporate Controller*, Jan./Feb. 1991.
2. CAM–I Glossary, *Journal of Cost Management*, Vol. 5 No. 3., Fall 1991, 58.
3. CAM–I Glossary, 57.
4. Robin Cooper and Peter B. B. Turney, "Tektronix: Portable Instruments Division (A, B, & C)," Harvard Business School, 1988.
5. Lou F. Jones, "Product Costing at Caterpillar," *Management Accounting*, Feb. 1991, 34–42.
6. Brent Nicholls, "ABC in the UK—A Status Report," *Management Accounting*, (UK), May 1992, 22.
7. CAM–I Glossary, 61.
8. David E. Keys, "Tracing Costs in the Three Stages of Activity-Based Management," *Journal of Cost Management*, Winter 1994, 30–37.
9. For a more in-depth discussion on life-cycle costing, see CAM–I's initial conceptual design, edited by Callie Berliner and James A. Brimson, published as *Cost Management for Today's Advanced Manufacturing*, Harvard Business School Press, 1988, 140.
10. For a description of software packages, see James P. Borden, "Activity-Based Management Software," *Journal of Cost Management*, Winter 1994, 39–49.
11. Michael C. O'Guin, *The Complete Guide to Activity-Based Costing*, (Englewood Cliffs, NJ: Prentice-Hall, 1991), 123.
12. Keith J. Williams, director of finance and accounting, Deere & Co., Mannheim, Germany.

3

MOVING FROM
PILOT TO MAINSTREAM

STEVE PLAYER AND DAVID E. KEYS

Perhaps the biggest development in ABM of late is the change in the way in which it is being used. Previous applications have illustrated its use as a cost reduction tool, as support for a one-time study, or in a pilot mode. We increasingly see ABM moving to the mainstream and being embedded as part of the ongoing management process.

Clear examples of where this has already occurred include Hewlett-Packard North American Distribution Organization (Chapter 4), Current, Inc. (Chapter 8), The Marmon Group (Chapter 9), Bliss & Laughlin Industries (Chapter 10), American Express (Chapter 12), and AT&T Paradyne (Chapter 14). These companies are blazing new trails and asking new questions.

- What process will be used to update the system data?
- What frequency is required and who funds it?
- What reporting enhancements should be made?
- What user training is needed to maximize use of the system?
- What type of organization is necessary to support the system? What skills sets? What functional expertise?
- How can we expand the system's usage?

To help understand the migration to mainstream systems, we have also included Appendix III, the "Stages of Cost and Performance Measurement Systems Development." This chart, along with Exhibit 1–4, "Illustrating the Overall Analytical Reporting Vision," provide a clearer view of what mainstream systems need to do and how you can migrate into them.

But to reach the point of asking these questions and needing this vision, a company must successfully negotiate the final ten pitfalls in moving from pilot to mainstream.

The pitfalls in going mainstream are behavioral (see Exhibit 3–1). Although all of the participants in the book's research project agreed that the technical pitfalls are important, participants with more experience implementing and using ABM identified and emphasized the behavioral pitfalls. Because they were not anticipated by early adopters of ABM, these pitfalls have not been documented comprehensively.

Exhibit 3-1

Pitfalls in Moving from Pilot to Mainstream

Pitfall #21	"I'm afraid, but I don't know it."
Pitfall #22	"We're afraid, but we don't know it."
Pitfall #23	"Wait a minute—this is messing with some long-held beliefs."
Pitfall #24	"What a world."
Pitfall #25	"Oh, yeah, do something with the numbers."
Pitfall #26	"Who wrote this, the legal department?"
Pitfall #27	"We were supposed to get this report two months ago."
Pitfall #28	"They're overhead."
Pitfall #29	"Times are good—why bother?"
Pitfall #30	"This will cost a fortune to operate."

Pitfall #21: "I'm afraid, but I don't know it."

Personal resistance to change is the first behavioral barrier to ABM implementation. And, to some degree, each of the other elements of collective resistance to change also rest on an individual element. The cause: inertia.

Inertia is a force that works on people's attitudes and actions just as it does on bodies of matter. The result is a tendency to resist any change (even one *known* to be beneficial). One underlying cause of resistance is the safety of the status quo. Individuals find comfort in the current state because they have survived it, which in turn magnifies the risk of the unknown that a major change may represent.

Both attitude and productivity sharply decline over time as people face change (see Exhibit 3-2). This is due to extra time and effort needed to learn the improvement method as well as the distress caused by realizing that others may perform at a higher level. This is particularly true if the company is profitable, an industry leader, or experiencing little or no competitive pressures. To a large degree, it is also true in organizations that are not doing well so long as the performance problems do not pose a direct, recognizable threat to individuals.

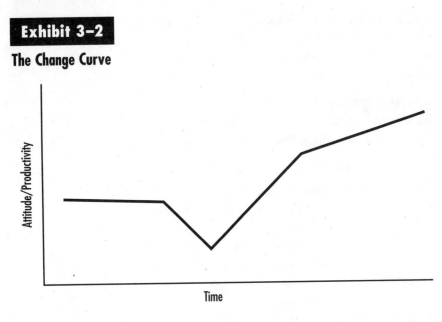

Exhibit 3-2

The Change Curve

The pitfall is failing to realize that change is nearly always met with resistance—and immediate action is required to overcome this resistance quickly. Individual resistance due to fear often becomes acute during attempts to move from pilot to mainstream.

This same type of resistance may have been encountered during the pilot, but at that stage it is usually easily overcome. The term "pilot" implies an experiment, something that will come and go. And in many cases, individual employees have very little understanding of how the pilot might affect their jobs, enabling them to view the pilot more as a curiosity than a threat. When the company begins to suggest moving from pilot to mainstream, a much greater degree of fear and resistance take hold.

Many things may combine to cause such fear. A simple fear of the unknown is one. Fear of what they don't understand is another. Some may fear that their own performances will be viewed differently.

For many managers, shifting to an ABM system is like playing a familiar game by the rules only to look up and find out that someone instituted a new way to score points. The individuals most proficient at following the old rules tend to give the greatest resistance to making changes.

Some product line managers may personally fear potential negative impacts to their product lines if they prove to be too costly. Such a result would make it more difficult for the product manager to show superior performance.

In addition, employees may be concerned about losing their jobs. Being asked to describe what work you do can often put people on the defensive. Teams must describe the process freely and completely to ensure that it is perceived properly. These actions can pave the way to implementation.

Fears of the unknown pose another risk. They have a way of magnifying any other problems that are encountered. If a team has difficulty gathering activity driver data, the mainstream effort may be overwhelmed by fears of massive data collection. Rumors of long update times on ABM software can sometimes lead to a pilot being scrapped even if those issues have already been corrected.

This pitfall often shows up in subtle ways. One key to overcoming these fears is training, particularly role play in developing, understanding, and using the data. Case exercises give employees hands-on experience, and keeping them posted as the pilot is developed prevents surprises.

Another technique to use is benchmarking visits. These meetings show managers that ABM can be done. There is comfort in talking to someone who has been there. CAM–I's CMS program helps to facilitate these types of discussions, and the Arthur Andersen ABO Continuum^{SM} (see Exhibit 1–2) helps mid-level management progress through the steps of awareness, buy-in, and ownership.

The key is to realize that fears are not numbers. They exist even though their composite magnitude cannot be seen. But an acknowledged fear can be dealt with swiftly and with strong measures. Making both strengths and weaknesses clear from the beginning helps people to view ABM realistically so that they can use ABM more effectively.

Pitfall #22: "We're afraid, but we don't know it."

A second type of resistance to implementing an ABM system comes from the departmental levels of an organization. ABM normally assigns costs to activities, then from activities to products through processes (or other cost objects). Traditional cost accounting systems collect costs by departments as part of the functional organization. Costs are then charged from departments to products.

ABM tends to ignore the functional organization of the company in making assignments to activities and to products or customers. While ABM yields valuable information about activities, it does not normally focus on departmental information, except for activity-based budgeting uses.

Many ABM systems define activities on an interdepartmental level, deliberately ignoring the functional departments that are used to run the organization. While interdepartmental teams and activities can be valuable, ignoring the functional organization of the company presents a clear danger to the success of ABM.

Departmental groups may view ABM as a threat. Some of these groups fear a loss of power, prestige, and importance to the company. Many fear that ABM information may be used to decrease the size of a department or even result in outsourcing the entire department. Department heads will perceive this potential loss of power and may attempt to subvert the ABM system.[1]

One area that is particularly sensitive to departmental resistance is the use of attribute flags to classify activity costs. Many managers may totally agree with the concept yet reject the results determined by its application. For example, value-added analysis may show that 80 percent of all costs in a particular area are spent on non-value-added activities. If managers are comfortable with the status quo, they may not believe that the status quo is so wasteful. The manager of such an area may become defensive, viewing ABM as a threat rather than a useful tool.

Activities can be defined on an intradepartmental level.[2] If intradepartmental definition is performed, departmental cost information can be generated by merely rolling up the cost of all activities within a department. This approach provides both activity and departmental information. However, it requires activities to be identified on a more detailed level. It also requires additional steps to ensure that interdepartmental activities can still be identified.

Another approach is to assign the cost of activities that are identified at an interdepartmental level to departments. However, this approach adds another layer of cost assignment to the ABM system.

Pitfall #23: "Wait a minute—this is messing with some long-held beliefs."

Cultural or societal beliefs can form a powerful barrier to implementation of an ABM system. Activity analysis and activity-based product costing provide a new and different view of an organization and its performance. Agreeing to use these new views may require a fairly radical departure from the viewpoint instilled by traditional systems.

In many cases, cost accounting systems are very old (some are more than 60 years old) and deeply entrenched. They may be the original systems since the company's inception. In fact, the fundamental workings of traditional cost accounting systems are still being taught in most colleges and universities. These two factors reinforce older mental models of how cost behavior should be viewed. They remain embedded in the subconscious even if they are known to be poor reflections of economic reality.

Invisible though they are, these cumulative life experiences form the foundation for the beliefs and value systems of a company, which will have a significant impact on how an ABM system will be received and what implementation steps will be required. At Hewlett-Packard, it means ABM implementation must conform to the consensus-building approach known internally as the H-P Way. At Texas Instruments, it means that deployment follows many pilots, which are responsive to each unit's needs.

Corporate beliefs shape how much a corporation is willing to share its ABM efforts. Members of CAM–I have advantages in rolling out ABM because their implementation teams share their experiences with each other. Other companies choose to be more secretive, believing that their ABM knowledge gives them a competitive advantage. The decision to opt for openness or secrecy is shaped by corporate culture.

Changing beliefs and value systems is seldom achieved overnight. In many cases, a crisis makes change to ABM irrefutable. Harris Semiconductor, a division of Harris Corporation, was facing severe financial pressure from global competition. New senior management helped create the opportunity to radically change existing systems and approaches to meet these threats. As a result, the Harris Semiconductor team implemented an ABM system on a worldwide basis in eight months (faster than some companies implement a pilot). Their situation created a unique opportunity to overcome these barriers.

Crisis situation or pure continuous improvement, people are still important. People support what they help create. People who will be using the system should be involved in its creation through techniques such as the Rapid Vision^{SM} storyboarding process.

ABM teams have also found it easier to link with a company's culture and beliefs rather than to try to steamroll them. Many identify the changes that need to be made by preparing a force-field analysis to articulate the forces that will help the implementation of ABM occur; they also note the forces that will restrain it.

From the analysis, plans can be made to start changing peoples' beliefs and value systems. With the tools to enable change, individuals' attitudes and productivity will recover and move to higher levels. These enablers include benchmarking and reward systems that minimize the length of time in the change curve. They also include training and communication that minimize the depth of decline in morale and productivity (see Exhibit 3–3). Though major change may take time, it is important to remember that a five-degree change in the rudder of the Exxon *Valdez* could have prevented the Alaskan disaster.

Exhibit 3-3

The Change Curve

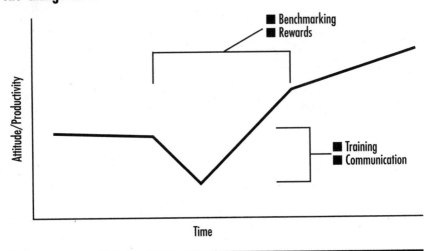

Pitfall #24: "What a world."

The business and regulatory environment can act as a significant barrier to successful implementation of ABM. In different environments individuals and groups with the same cultural background may react differently to change. Sometimes the environment is an important factor in an organization's decision to even start ABM. Whatever the situation, organizations may not realize the full significance of potential environmental problems until ABM is underway.

The legal climate and governmental regulations of each country in which the organization does business can have a profound effect on whether ABM is successful as well. Companies in the United States that are considering adoption of ABM have encountered not only generally accepted accounting principles (GAAP), but also potential implications with governmental regulations of the Department of Defense, Medicare, and Medicaid.

The use of GAAP for external financial reporting purposes is perhaps the most pervasive environmental factor affecting successful ABM implementations. These rules, developed almost exclusively for the financial view of costs, have resulted in many companies implementing GAAP-driven ABC systems. One accountant who was responsible for implementing ABC was told by a straight-faced CEO, "You can do anything you want, just as long as it is GAAP!" His attitude, of course, prevented the ABC system from even coming close to achieving it's full potential.

ABM systems that are implemented independent of GAAP will normally be in violation of GAAP rules for several reasons. They include:

- ABM systems will assign some selling and administrative costs to products;
- ABM will not assign some manufacturing costs to products (e.g., plant manager's salary, plant security, and retiree health care costs caused by decisions in prior years);
- ABM's ability to span time periods to compute life-cycle costs;
- ABM's flexibility to include imputed interest costs in inventory; and
- ABM's ability to use replacement cost and units of production methods of depreciating fixed assets.

The solution to the GAAP-related problem is to implement a stand-alone ABC system or adjust the ABC system for differences with GAAP. The users of GAAP and ABC information are different, their purposes are different, and their time frames and reporting frequencies are different. Why should it be insisted that their costs be the same?

Large government contractors selling to the Department of Defense (DOD) are required to comply with Federal Acquisitions Regulations, laws that require contractors to share cost and pricing data with the DOD. As a result, a huge environmental barrier is created due to defense contractors' fear that data from a mainstream ABC system would fall under this cost and pricing data disclosure requirement.

Even though the government has urged contractors to move forward with ABC systems, most contractors have refrained from implementing mainstream systems. These contractors fear that contracting officers will cherry pick from the ABC results, selecting to impose lower contract prices on any contracts being overcosted while not agreeing to increase those that are undercosted. The fear is particularly acute when a contractor is serving multiple branches of the military and therefore drawing from different budget lines. Government contractors' fear is a major reason that most of them have not tried to implement mainstream systems.

Health care providers often have similar concerns. Reimbursement for health care costs by governmental agencies is often related to costs through the use of diagnostic-related groups. For example, if a health care provider can prove that a certain procedure costs more than the standard reimbursement for that diagnostic-related group, then the reimbursement will be increased. If the ABC on a diagnostic procedure is less than it is in the traditional system, the amount of the reimbursement for the procedure could be lost.

Solutions to overcoming environmental barriers often lie outside of a company's control. The aerospace and defense interest group within CAM–I's CMS

program has been used to create dialogue between the government and its contractors. Unfortunately the level of mistrust has not been overcome. Actual
changes in the regulations may be necessary to remove this barrier.

Presently, many government contractors are effectively using ABM systems,
but with a different focus. Those using ABM have shifted to the operational
view using the techniques to support reengineering and other major cost reduction efforts.

Pitfall #25: "Oh, yeah, do something with the numbers."

Probably the most surprising pitfall in implementing ABM is that managers
often will not take action once they receive ABM information. For example,
managers do not act to eliminate activities. Marketing refuses to change prices.
And, no attempts are made to modify cost drivers.

Even if the ABM system has been used to generate insightful information,
no benefit is derived until managers act on that information. If accountants
developed the ABM system, they often overemphasize the importance of the
accounting numbers and underemphasize the importance of why the numbers
were generated in the first place. One accountant told us, "People get so
involved in the mechanism of ABM that they lose sight of using it to make decisions." Another said, "Accountants are so excited about how good the information is that they think their work is finished and no further action is required."

This is one of the main reasons that some consultants continue to modify
their approaches to ABM, changing their technique in several ways:

- First, more emphasis is placed on the client's personnel being involved in
  developing ABM.
- Second, more emphasis is placed on training managers on how to use the
  information.
- Third, specific objectives are set for the ABM system, taking into consideration the decisions that will use the ABM information.
- Fourth, certain managers are targeted to use the ABM information.
- Fifth, a champion of the ABM system is selected who will use ABM and
  encourage others to use it.
- Sixth, a pilot ABM system might be targeted to generate information for
  specific decisions so that early successes can be achieved.

Companies experiencing this pitfall need to start with the business issues
that ABM seeks to address. Managers then identify what decisions the ABM system will influence and who will use the information to make those decisions.
This information, along with key tasks, the people responsible for completing

the tasks, and expected completion dates, is summarized into an implementation action plan. Simple planning tools like this can create powerful results and ensure avoidance of this pitfall.

Pitfall #26: "Who wrote this, the legal department?"

Too often, accountants prepare reports that use unnecessarily complex accounting terminology, which can only be understood by other accountants, and include too much information. Reports that are difficult to understand are limited in their use and do not reflect favorably on the financial department. They merely mean the accountant developing the report was not trained well enough to prepare it in a manner that could be easily understood. A mistake far too common in traditional cost systems, it also occurs too frequently in ABM reports.

Most off-the-shelf ABM software packages lack comprehensive, easy-to-understand reporting. Their user group meetings are often clustered with discussions of how to make the system's output more flexible and user friendly. Many people work around this problem by writing output files to spreadsheets or database files.

In almost every company that was included in our research effort, the accountants thought their reports were more useful than did the users of those reports. Accountants talked about how much information was on reports and how many people received each report. Users of the reports talked about understanding neither the reports nor the accountants' explanations of the reports. Users also frequently mentioned that they did not use the reports.

Two companies that are direct competitors had completely different approaches on this issue. One company's cost accountants were very proud of their numerous and very detailed reports. On first glance, none of their reports could be understood. An expert in each report had to spend a good deal of time explaining the information that was in each report so that it could be understood.

The other company, which has a successful ABM system, showed us its basic ABC report on the cost of a part. It could be understood without any explanation. Direct and indirect costs, activity drivers, activity driver rates, and activity pools were clearly and concisely presented on the report. If you were a manager, which type of report would you rather receive?

To correct the problem, accountants must ask some key questions. Who are the users of ABM reports? What information do they need and want? Have the reports been explained to the users so they can understand them? To find the answers, accountants will have to get out of their offices, observe what is going on, and talk to the users of their reports.

One idea being used by some companies is to limit financial reports to one page. While supporting schedules with more detail are allowed, the purpose is to aggregate all relevant information in an easily understandable format using simple and clear terminology on one page.

Pitfall #27: "We were supposed to get this report two months ago."

Traditional cost systems are typically used to generate monthly reports as well as annual reports. Comparisons of actual costs with budgeted departmental or standard costs and the resulting variance analysis are done monthly. If operational performance reports are prepared, they are usually prepared on a monthly cycle. If management finds monthly reports to be untimely, the normal response is to implement a summarized flash report one day after month end or to begin daily or weekly sales reporting.

When a company adopts ABM, a decision has to be made about whether to link these reports with ABM. Since the old cost system generated this information, many managers believe ABM should also generate this information. However, ABM is much more detailed than the traditional system, so preparation of these monthly reports on an ABM basis is much more time consuming and costly to generate.

Some managers view reporting as a once-a-year snapshot rather than an ongoing monthly system. Their focus is generally on product costing. Performance reporting for short-term operational control is not a focus of the ABM system they envision. Companies using this approach use semiannual or annual updates of reports to provide information for longer-term decisions such as product pricing, customer profitability, and activity analysis.

For short-term control, managers reported that monthly (or even more frequent) variances are of limited usefulness. The variances (computed on either an ABM basis or a traditional basis) are reported not only after operations have taken place, but also after an accountant takes time (e.g., one week) to receive and process the information. This is similar to waiting until one week after a battle is over to count the bodies. The information is not very useful in limiting the number of deaths during the battle.

The key to avoiding these problems is to link the frequency of reporting with the three views of costs (see Exhibit 1–3). The strategic view of costs is consistent with semiannual or annual reports. More frequent reporting is unnecessary. The operational view of costs requires immediate feedback. Physical measures are reported hourly or daily.

The operational view of costs can be integrated with Just-in-Time (JIT) and total quality management (TQM). JIT and TQM give managers ideal goals to be continuously pursued with almost instantaneous feedback on a very desegregated level. For example, the use of control charts in statistical process control allows process operators to get immediate feedback on the specific causes of problems. The elimination of these problems results in lower costs as well as higher quality and lower cycle time.

Pitfall #28: "They're overhead."

One surprising behavioral pitfall to implementing ABM is how many subunits of the organization in which ABM is implemented are not profit centers. As such, all of their costs are passed on and profitability is not a concern. Someone higher in the chain of command makes pricing, product mix, and other revenue decisions. If ABC is implemented at a plant that is a cost center, managers at the cost center often fail to perceive what benefits ABC could provide. These managers are normally evaluated on how their actual costs compare to budgets. They are responsible for the efficient production of output, but are not evaluated on profit. These managers focus on operational cost. Although these managers could use ABM information to generate cost savings, they would not receive any benefit from using ABC information for pricing and product or product line profitability decisions.

Managers of such cost centers may not fully understand the importance of decisions made based on ABM information. Since ABM requires that local managers provide more time and support, they resist its usage. Why should local managers support a cost system that does little to help them? What benefit is derived from providing detailed data for decisions made elsewhere? While this may seem to be a short-sighted case, many participants cited it as a problem.

A simple way to avoid this pitfall is to focus implementation at the profit center level. Another approach is to have cost centers price their output costs and benchmark it against market rates, which can create profit center type thinking even though earning a profit is not required.

Finally, implementation of market-based, or target costing, pushes the notion of affordable costs down into the cost centers, allowing for clear insights into which plants are contributing to the value of the organization and which are consuming or degrading the organization's value.

Pitfall #29: "Times are good—why bother?"

Some companies that are profitable do not see the need to improve. To them, ABM represents a change from the status quo, and the status quo is pretty good.

While ABM can help companies that are under severe competitive pressure become more profitable, it can also help companies that aren't under fire become even more profitable. Therefore, high profit levels are not a valid reason for not using ABM.

General Electric is a prime example of a profitable company that continues to seek ways to improve. The roots of activity analysis can be traced to approaches pioneered by General Electric in the 1960s. This approach of continuous improvement means that a successful organization constantly looks for ways to perform at a higher level. It does not mean that a company stops running to turn around and watch its competitors catch up. A continuously improving company seeks to not only maintain its lead but to increase it.

Profitable companies can use ABM information to benchmark performance against best practices for each key process regardless of the industry. The use of benchmarking in this manner changes the focus from "we are the best in our industry" to "we can do better."

Pitfall #30: "This will cost a fortune to operate."

While the initial cost of an ABM system is one issue, the cost of maintaining an ABM system can be an even bigger one. Mistakes will be found in the ABM system and will need to be corrected. Suggestions for improvements will be identified and need to be incorporated. Consideration should be given to automating the input of driver data, a step that, if taken, will require training of users. As an organization changes, its ABM system will need to be modified to reflect these changes. As an organization's activities change and as the causes of its costs change, the ABM system must be updated. Since organizations are currently changing very rapidly due to downsizing, reengineering, TQM, etc., the number of changes and the related cost of keeping the ABM system current can become substantial.

For example, an ABM system may include ten activity drivers while the traditional system only had direct labor as an overhead base. Keeping these drivers current can be significantly more expensive than tracking direct labor. Companies that had trouble keeping direct labor standards current should study the ongoing commitment costs of ABM before adopting it. As noted before, these costs are only justified by the value of the decisions that companies make with them. Be sure that the ABM system is used to make the right decisions, otherwise the costs of developing and maintaining the ABM system will be wasted.

Also keep in mind that in some advanced implementations, direct labor reporting as we know it today has been discontinued, and the ABM reporting that replaced it was less expensive and more relevant.

Solutions

After many years of worthwhile experiments, it's clear that ABM is here to stay. Because it works, the companies are making ABM the heart of their decision support systems and rethinking how legacy systems are designed and maintained. With the power of the current database programs and the availability of many platform options, nearly any cost management vision can become a reality.

SUMMARY
Pitfall #21: "I'm afraid, but I don't know it."

Symptoms

- Individuals cannot clearly state what benefits an ABM system will provide them, but they are very clear on the effort it will require.
- Presentation of ABM data is politely received, but managers continue to behave in the same manner as before.
- Managers emphasize how successful the company has been without ABM.
- Passive or active resistance comes from product managers whose products appear to be undercosted.
- People understate the problems with the old cost accounting system.
- People understate the benefits of ABM.

Treatment

- Articulate the expected benefits from ABM in written form. Show what business objectives and issues it will address.
- Train employees on how ABM will be used. Explain what role they will play. Ask them to articulate how it will affect their jobs.
- Publish summaries of the problems and benefits of both the new ABM and the old traditional system.
- Deal with product line issues by enlisting the aid of those product managers whose products appear to be overcosted.
- Challenge people to justify their comments.

Pitfall #22: "We're afraid, but we don't know it."

Symptoms

- Departmental groups resist implementing the ABM system.
- The ABM system no longer provides previously available departmental information.
- Functional groups cling to the vertical organizational structure. There is a lack of horizontal coordination between departments.
- Functional groups fear that the ABM system will be used to eliminate the group.

Treatment
- Train departments on how ABM will be used. Discuss its potential impacts on the company and each particular department.
- Modify the ABM system to enable it to provide departmental information or retain visibility of departmental data through use of account codes.
- Identify activities at an intradepartmental level.
- Decrease the emphasis on the functional organization by requiring identification of internal suppliers and customers in a horizontal process.

Pitfall #23: "Wait a minute—this is messing with some long-held beliefs."

Symptoms
- Managers repeatedly asked for the same reports that came from the old traditional system.
- Subconscious norms affect how people view cost information.
- People assume that the ABM system has the same problems as the prior approaches without even reviewing it.
- People fear uncertainty.

Treatment
- Give each person sufficient training. Involve employees in selection of activities and cost drivers.
- Have people complete surveys about beliefs at the start of training. Discuss survey results.
- Obtain top management commitment and support in changing the beliefs.
- Identify any crisis that can be used to speed implementation.
- Prepare a force-field analysis showing what beliefs and values will support the ABM implementation and which ones will oppose it.
- Implement and emphasize continuous improvement.

Pitfall #24: "What a world."

Symptoms
- Regulatory authorities are inflexible.
- Fear exists that regulatory agencies will cherry pick the results from the ABM cost systems, yielding a lower net recovery.
- Regulatory authorities will not discuss concerns of the regulated companies.

Treatment
- Develop internal expertise in relevant regulations.
- Communicate concerns to regulatory authorities.

- Seek legal advice to better understand legal issues and to identify possible alternatives.
- Reach a written agreement with the regulatory authority on how the potential impacts of ABC system will be treated.
- Help change regulations to remove the barrier.

Pitfall #25: "Oh, yeah, do something with the numbers."

Symptoms
- The accountants who develop ABM overemphasize the importance of the accounting numbers and fail to remember the purpose for generating the numbers in the first place.
- Marketing refuses to change prices.
- No activities are eliminated. Cost drivers are not evaluated.
- No one takes ownership for using the system in decision making. No one owns the decision.

Treatment
- Develop a written plan for how the system will affect decision making. Note what the decisions are, how the system will help in making them, whose responsibility they are, and when they will be made.
- Monitor the number of changes that are made using ABM information.
- Require managers to justify inaction as well as action.
- Involve users of information in the ABM system as soon as possible.
- Train expected users on the system. Include specific examples of how ABM information can be used for decisions (e.g., pricing and cost savings) in training sessions.

Pitfall #26: "Who wrote this, the legal department?"

Symptoms
- Managers do not read the reports. They do not contain the information that managers need or want.
- Accountants do not talk with users. Operational personnel do not understand accounting reports.
- Accountants do not understand the business in operational terms. They can only talk in financial terms.
- Reports are too long. They include too many numbers.
- Unnecessary accounting terminology is used in reports.

Treatment
- Move accountants' offices into the plant (closer to users of reports).
- Survey users of accounting information to determine clarity, conciseness, and understandability of reports. Ask if reports meet managers' needs.
- Ask users of accounting information to explain the information.
- Set a one-page limit for each report.
- Give accountants TQM training.

Pitfall #27: "We were supposed to get this report two months ago."

Symptoms
- Managers are seeking ABC reports on a monthly basis to replace those generated by the traditional cost system.
- Variances are used for short-term cost control.
- Requests are made to increase the frequency of reports.
- The relationship between ABC and the short-term operational control system is not understood. Strategically focused systems are expected to provide operational control.

Treatment
- Have managers examine the three views of costs. Focus reporting frequency on the required view.
- Prepare strategic costing reports on a semiannual or annual cycle. Implement a sales pricing tool for "what if" pricing analysis.
- Operational reports can be issued by people in the operation rather than by accountants. Base reports on physical rather than financial measures.
- Define and clearly specify the relationship between the ABM system and the views of costs it will try to support.

Pitfall #28: "They're overhead."

Symptoms
- Cost center managers are not concerned with product pricing issues.
- Managers ignore the interrelationships of functional areas of the company. They focus only on gathering the information necessary to optimize their individual unit's performance.
- Managers worry only about how events affect themselves.
- Excessive emphasis is placed on cost reduction rather than increasing profits.

Treatment

- Implement ABM at the profit center level (e.g., broaden the pilot to include revenue responsibility).
- Include overall company profitability in everyone's performance measures and reward structure.
- Share information (e.g., profit and subunit profitability) with managers who have only cost responsibility.
- Place more emphasis on increasing long-term profits and less emphasis on short-run cost reduction.
- Explore the use of target costing to provide market focus to cost centers.

Pitfall #29: "Times are good—why bother?"

Symptoms

- Managers do not see the need to improve. They are happy with the status quo.
- The company does not use continuous improvement.
- Managers are happy with the current level of profits.
- Managers do not feel an immediate competitive threat.

Treatment

- Review a list of the top 100 most profitable companies from 10, 20, and 30 years ago. Note where they are today.
- Focus discussions on the benefits of ABM in identifying future sources of competitive advantage.
- Benchmark against best practices whether they are in the same industry or not.
- Benchmark subunits of the organization against other subunits.

Pitfall #30: "This will cost a fortune to operate."

Symptoms

- Previous spending on the old cost accounting system was limited, as standards were not updated on a regular basis.
- Driver data collection is primarily manual.
- No provision has been made for regular updating of the ABM information.
- ABM information must be changed frequently to reflect the multitude of changes in the organization.
- No formal system exists for documenting suggestions for improvement in the ABM system.

Treatment

- Articulate what decisions the ABM system is expected to help make. Quantify the expected value or benefit of those decisions. Compare this to the projected maintenance costs.
- Consider simplifying the ABM system by decreasing the number of activities, resource drivers, and cost drivers included in the system.
- Update the strategic ABC system annually. Update process cost tables more frequently to support operational decisions. Focus on which view of cost and frequency are required.
- Implement a formal system for documenting errors and suggestions for improvements to the ABM system.

Notes

1. David E. Keys and Robert J. LeFevre, "Departmental Activity-Based Management," *Management Accounting* (forthcoming) and Brent Nicholls, "ABC in the UK—A Status Report," *Management Accounting* (U.K.), May 1992, 22.
2. Keys and LeFevre.

Section II

Case Studies

4

DISTRIBUTION: KNOWING WHAT IT TAKES— AND WHAT IT COSTS

Hewlett-Packard–North American
Distribution Organization, Santa Clara, California

STEVE PLAYER, CATHIE WIER, AND CRAIG R. COLLINS

*Steve Player is a Partner and Firmwide Director of
Cost Management with Arthur Andersen LLP in Dallas.*
Cathie Wier is a Senior Manager with Arthur Andersen LLP in San Jose.
Craig R. Collins is an Experienced Manager with Arthur Andersen LLP in Dallas.

SUMMARY

Business Issues

Hewlett-Packard needed more accurate business information to provide to its management and business partners.

Strategic decisions facing Hewlett-Packard:

■ what channels to emphasize;
■ what customers to emphasize;
■ which types of customer service to provide;
■ how to price those services; and
■ what is the optimal supplier-to-reseller configuration (should Hewlett-Packard act as an information highway only or as a physical transportation source)?

How ABC Was Used

■ The activity-based costing (ABC) model for Hewlett-Packard was developed to provide a better understanding of costs at Hewlett-Packard's North American Distribution Organization (HP–NADO).
■ The ABC model named SAM (Strategic Activity Management) by Hewlett-Packard provides both strategic and operational information including full customer segment costing, full product costing, simple process costing, and targeting of improvement opportunities.

Hewlett-Packard's Results

■ Product costing results showed major unintended subsidies of low-volume products.
■ Customer costing results showed dramatic differences in customer profitability.
■ Reengineering pilots used the ABC information to identify more than $2 million in potential savings.

The next time you shop for a computer or some piece of high-tech peripheral equipment, chances are your ultimate selection will be driven by two questions: what can it do for me and how much will it cost? As state-of-the-art electronics presses technology to dramatic dimensions of capabilities, prices for exotic devices seem to be continually decreasing. Who, then, is making a profit, and how?

Not too long ago, Hewlett–Packard's North American Distribution Organization (HP–NADO) asked itself the same questions and decided to use ABC to sort out the answers.

Hewlett-Packard, with revenues of $25 billion a year, is a world leader in manufacturing PCs, computer systems, printers, scanners, and work stations. It has four product distribution centers worldwide, with HP–NADO alone distributing 21 product lines (LaserJet, DeskJet, and the like) through six customer resale channels. In 1994, HP–NADO, headquartered in Santa Clara, California, distributed nearly $7 billion in products through five physical depots to more than 300 principal resellers nationwide.

Hewlett-Packard's Business Environment

In Hewlett-Packard's manufacturing process, outside suppliers from multiple global locations ship raw materials, components, and other parts to primary manufacturing plants. The Hewlett-Packard plants then produce standardized versions of the various elements of Hewlett-Packard's product lines. The elements are shipped to HP–NADO and other depots for customization to specific geographic markets (called localization), packaging, and shipping to Hewlett-Packard's main reseller channels. With potential customization steps numbering in the hundreds or thousands, the huge volume of products, the myriad individual back-end costs to make and service, the diversity of products, and various customer-market channels, record keeping can be very complex.

Hewlett-Packard had a costing process of multiple allocations that spread overhead charges across the entire organization. But the company needed a means for generating more accurate business information about HP–NADO's costs, including how these costs influence the company's profitability (the strategic view of costs) and how the data could be used to identify opportunities for cost reduction in selected areas (the operational view of costs).

Strategic Activity Management (SAM)

In January 1994, Arthur Andersen was engaged to help Hewlett-Packard implement an ABC program that would cover the costs of the entire HP–NADO operation—from front-end order-taking and administration to back-end assembly and distribution. Teaming up with HP–NADO finance, the project team named the project Strategic Activity Management (SAM), and set out to understand the costs that contributed to product and customer profitability. (A subsequent Hewlett-Packard project using a similar ABC approach devoted to the financial view of costs was also implemented. It was nicknamed "Son of SAM.")

The SAM project broke new ground in both modeling and analysis of the ABC/ABM information. Although developers of ABM pilots are generally warned not to take on too much, there was a strong desire at Hewlett-Packard to understand both product and customer profitability simultaneously, including an understanding of the interrelationships of these cost objects (see Exhibit 4–1). So the project focused on both product and customer costs and aimed to determine the contribution of these costs to product and customer profitability.

The analysis of product costs ultimately revealed that many of Hewlett-

Exhibit 4-1

The Slice & Dice Cube

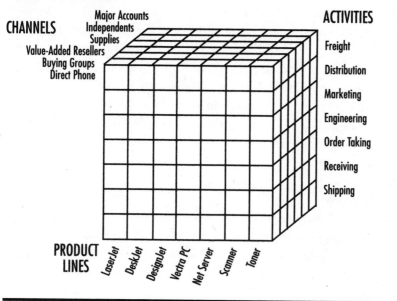

Packard's lower volume products were actually being subsidized by their higher volume counterparts. The customer cost analysis showed dramatic differences in the costs of providing service to HP–NADO's six different customer channels, as well as the customers within those channels. An interesting aspect of the analysis relates to the service requirements a customer demands for the product mix and volume purchased. This ratio ultimately drives the customer's profitability profile.

Most manufacturers know down to the penny the costs of producing their products. But many variables (such as colors, capabilities, packaging, delivery, and service) arise when selling specialized products to individual customers. SAM helped HP–NADO focus on finding the real costs of these differences and determining the impact they had on the company's earnings.

The ABC Strategy

At the outset, HP–NADO identified specific issues it needed to address, including:

- which channels to emphasize;
- which customers to emphasize;
- which customer services to provide;

- how to price those services; and
- how to determine the optimal supplier-to-reseller configuration.

Besides these issues, it was clear that the model and the information available from the model would be used for more than just a strategic view of costs and profitability. It would be used to initiate process improvement and reengineering. Understanding the processes that contributed to the costs of the products and customer channels was an integral part of the project. With that understanding, HP–NADO could identify which processes to reengineer or improve. It was clear at the onset that information about product and customer costs alone would not be enough to improve HP–NADO's profitability; process changes had to happen.

Vital Statistics

The project team was highly leveraged. Seven full-time team members from Hewlett-Packard's finance staff and the equivalent of $2^{1}/_{2}$ team members from Arthur Andersen's Advanced Cost Management Team (see Exhibit 4–2) were helped by technical experts who trained the team and addressed difficult modeling issues.

Exhibit 4–2

SAM Project Team Composition

Hewlett-Packard Staff Members
Chris Marino, PC Business Materials Manager and Project Leader
Scott Putz, Financial Analyst and Team Coordinator
Michael Bordoni, Financial Operations Manager
Cindy Gion, Financial Operations Manager
Tami Read, Senior Financial Analyst
James Schinella, Supplies Business Distribution Programs Manager
Irene Suzuki, Retail Segment Order Fulfillment Supervisor

Arthur Andersen's Advanced Cost Management Team Members
Dan St. Peter, Project Partner
Steve Player, Partner and Firmwide Director of Cost Management
Cathie Wier, Senior Manager and Model Design Consultant
Craig R. Collins, Manager
Julie Debenham, Senior Consultant

The Process

The project launched ABC into all areas of HP–NADO in a 3¹/₂-month time frame—without a pilot. Suffice it to say that implementation was conducted at a breakneck pace.

The process began using the storyboarding technique, in which groups of HP–NADO employees or even whole departments were brought together to discuss their operations. Initial team training was provided by Arthur Andersen's Mark Moelling, who was one of the first to apply storyboarding to ABM implementation. Department teams wrote down on index cards all of their activities and noted their purpose, key activities, and supporting tasks (see Exhibit 4–3 for development statistics).

Exhibit 4–3

HP–NADO's SAM System Development Statistics

Storyboard Sessions	51
Functional Areas Covered	81
Key Activities Identified	527
Staff Included in Model	1,410
Drivers Utilized by Model	27
Processes Costed	180
Product Families Costed	55
Customers Costed	75

In the early stages of the project, the team asked questions about availability of data. Initial indications that the data already existed were overwhelming, leading team members to believe that driver data would be easy to pull together. In fact, much of the data was being maintained on several systems with various levels of aggregation. However, the effort needed to prepare the data for the model was a big surprise. Because of the many sources and formats of data, the process of collecting and converting the data for the first model was a major undertaking. Once the data sources were known and formats were understood, though, the process could be simplified.

As the project progressed, the volume of data gathered for SAM took on the shape of an inverted pyramid. The team identified 527 activities, from receipt of materials to billing customers, performed by HP–NADO employees. At the process level, the project team asked employees to describe their work in particular operations. The team traced activities to subprocesses and processes. The activities were then traced to products and customers. At the activity level, they accumulated voluminous data to get a better understanding of potential process improvements.

From the activity analysis, the SAM model became a targeting device for defining areas for concentrated study. An activity dictionary listed all activities performed at HP–NADO. The model provided a time and cost matrix of activities matched with all the employees who performed them. Then the activities were consolidated to process and subprocess levels. Additional analysis was added in the form of site costing, which allowed analysts to determine the cost of running each physical site.

Definition of an extremely large number of activities was helpful in understanding operational views of costs (for target cost reductions). However, such a large number can become overwhelming for strategic purposes. To address strategic questions, the activities were grouped by subprocesses and attributed to products and customers based on a more manageable number of activity drivers.

Identifying Model Alternatives

To facilitate the collection and analysis of labor costs, a Microsoft Access database served as a front-end preprocessor for the ABC model. Data was collected, consolidated, and formatted for import into EasyABC software. In fact, much of the detailed activity analysis was carried out in this Access database. Then, aggregated data was moved to the EasyABC model. The EasyABC model was small and agile even though the supporting database included massive detail about the individual activities and related costs (see Exhibit 4–4).

Building a model to both fully cost customers and fully cost products (all costs flowing to customers and all costs flowing to products for profitability analysis) was an interesting challenge. The average ABC model fully costs just one category of cost objects, usually products. When designing the model, the team came up with several alternatives.

One alternative was to attempt to analyze the profitability of products and customers within one model. The resulting design of the cost object module was complex. Costs flowed from activities to customers and products, then all product costs flowed to customers. Finally, those customer costs flowed to a second representation of all of the product costs on a fully loaded basis. In order to maintain the integrity of the activity data all the way through to the final cost objects, detailed accounts had to be maintained for each set of cost objects. The projected size of the model simply exploded. Although the costs could be calculated correctly, the need for simple analysis and quick calculations led the team to reject this approach.

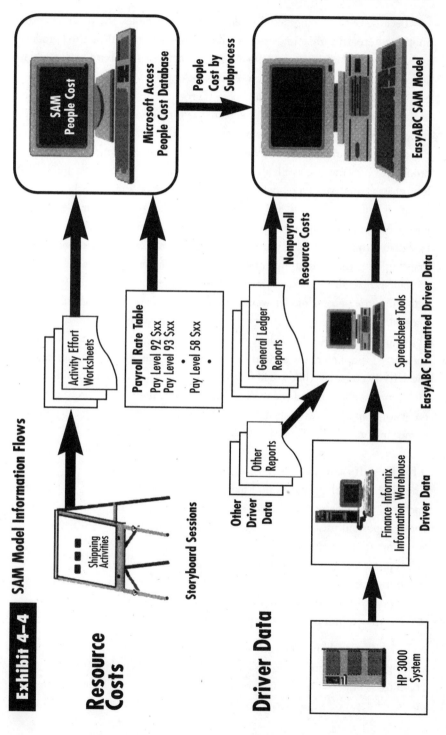

Exhibit 4–4 SAM Model Information Flows

Because of the strong desire to do it all in one model, the team looked at another alternative, this time using a bill of costs to roll up fully costed products and customers. If all resources were assigned to activities, activity costs could be added as a bill of activities to each of the cost objects. Although it would have been possible to generate both fully costed products and fully costed customers in this manner, it was essential to calculate the total costs and be able to analyze the contributions to those costs through all levels of assignment. (Note: When the model was built in March 1994, ABC Technologies' client server/network product OROS was not available. Through the use of OROS Links and OROS Reports, the analysis of a model using the bill of costs is simplified.)

This left one obvious and simple alternative. Create two models within EasyABC—one for customer profitability and the other for product profitability. Because the project team was just learning EasyABC, this was troublesome at first. Building and maintaining one model was a challenge, what would it mean to double the effort? The key to success was recognizing that once the first model was built, the second model would be relatively easy—both to build and to maintain. The structure of the two models differed only in the ultimate cost object module and in the assignments of only a very few activities. The team considered simplifying the second model (the customer model) by starting with the activity costs, but that would have meant that customer costs could not easily be analyzed in terms of the resources that contributed. Therefore, a complete replication approach was taken. (Note: With the release of OROS, the analysis of multiple models has been simplified.)

The Results for Hewlett-Packard

The SAM model provided information never before available to Hewlett-Packard's management. On the operational side, HP–NADO identified a number of important uses for the SAM model including:

- support of operational improvement teams;
- support for activity-based budgeting and flexible budgeting;
- using attributes to identify under what time frames costs vary;
- support of economic value analysis; and
- use in determining manager performance related to cost efficiency.

The data could now be reviewed in terms of the three views of costs: financial, operational, and strategic. The SAM model linked data from the storyboarding sessions with various functional groups, activities, business processes, product lines, and customer segments. It revealed opportunities to drill down into the data, as well as how different paper trails flowed throughout all levels of the organization.

To demonstrate how the SAM information could be used to target and achieve operational improvements, the team identified three pilot areas to re-engineer. These included sales order administration, physical warehouse activities, and information technology costs. The team examined where errors occurred and how to reduce cycle times and inventory requirements.

One pilot provided validation of a major change in the assembly of personal computers, which involved going from a build-to-stock environment to a build-to-order environment. Two other pilots offered new recommendations for operational improvements. Overall, the three pilots identified more than $2 million in potential savings for HP–NADO. While the SAM model's primary purpose is strategic cost information, these annual cost savings represent a significant short-term return on the costs invested.

The model's strategic value was even more far-reaching. From all of this data, the team ultimately learned that 51 customers, less than 10 percent of total customers, accounted for 85 percent of all HP–NADO's orders. The model proved to be a powerful tool for analyzing customer and channel profitability; developing contract discount structures; analyzing costs of key services; determining the impact of outsourcing distribution functions; determining the impact of outsourcing certain products or services; performing benchmarking of key areas; and using the model to help justify investment decisions.

LESSONS LEARNED

- ABC techniques can be used for both product and customer cost analyses.
- The flexibility of ABC allows implementers to design models to meet evolving needs.
- Building models to fully cost products and customers, meeting both operational and strategic goals is possible, though not recommended for pilot projects.
- Because of the extraordinary amount of information brought forth in the ABC process, it is important to allow sufficient time for data collection and analysis.
- Initiate gathering the activity-driver information early in the data gathering process. While information often already runs through transactional systems, it is rarely captured and summarized in the way needed for the ABC model.
- ABC proved to be a unique and powerful tool for looking simultaneously at the cost of processes, product lines, and customer segments.

5

A PROCESS MANUFACTURING COMPANY'S PRESCRIPTION FOR PROFITABILITY

Hoffmann-La Roche, Inc.
Nutley, New Jersey

ROBERT G. CUMMISKEY AND CHUCK MARX

Robert G. Cummiskey is a Manager with Arthur Andersen LLP in New York. Chuck Marx is a Partner with Arthur Andersen LLP in Chicago.

SUMMARY

Business Issues

Pharmaceutical companies today are under increasing pressure to reduce costs and respond to current health care reforms. Hoffmann-La Roche—Nutley, New Jersey, the largest subsidiary of the Swiss-based parent, is continually looking for ways to decrease costs while maintaining superior standards.

Hoffmann-La Roche needed a performance measurement system to identify process improvement opportunities and maintain an environment of continuous improvement.

How ABM Was Used

With much of the groundwork already completed by internal ABM experts, Hoffmann-La Roche asked Arthur Andersen to help set up a pilot ABM model. The objectives of the pilot were to train a team of employees to implement the process and demonstrate the benefits of the methodology to other parts of the company.

- The 15-member cross-functional team consisted of employees with both financial and operational backgrounds.
- Just-in-Time training was used to brief team members on various ABM phases immediately prior to performing the tasks.
- Frequent steering committee meetings with top management sustained and ensured executive support and enthusiasm.

Hoffmann-La Roche's Results

Upon completion of the eight-week pilot, the team had established a solid base of ABM expertise and organizational support. Now, leveraging off that base, the company is rolling out the process to other parts of the Nutley, New Jersey, facility.

- Responsibility for implementing improvement opportunities identified during the pilot have been assigned;
- Full implementation teams and plans have been established for the remainder of the functional areas included in the pilot and two additional functions;
- An ABM integration team has been formed to automate data collection and model updates; and
- A full-time ABM administrator has been designated.

With today's intense focus on health care reform and cost reduction, drug manufacturers are continually seeking new opportunities to lower costs while maintaining superior quality standards.

Hoffmann-La Roche, Inc. is no exception. With the parent company, Roche Holding, Ltd., headquartered in Basel, Switzerland, Hoffmann-La Roche has operations around the world. One of its premier facilities, in Nutley, New Jersey, about ten miles from New York City, quickly identified the need for cost alternatives in order to meet demands for lower prices.

Cost Improvement

Hoffmann-La Roche's biggest need was to put a process in place that would enable the company to first identify critical areas for improvement and then measure precisely what benefits those improvements had achieved. The company identified ABM as the process for continuous bottom-line impact and improvement.

Bob Fischetta, assistant controller and director of Technical Services for Hoffmann-La Roche, was first to introduce ABM to the organization. He gave numerous presentations and training sessions extolling the advantages of ABM; his knowledge of the methodology enabled him to convince senior management of ABM's many benefits.

Lou Schmukler, director of Pharmaceutical Operations, also had previous ABM experience and joined Fischetta in his efforts to promote its use. Schmukler kept the resources for the project focused and moving in the right direction—forward. This blend of financial and operational executive support laid the foundation for a successful project. Hoffmann-La Roche had full executive support and a 15-member cross-functional team in place to begin the engagement. At that point, the company called in Arthur Andersen and Sapling Corporation, the producers of Net Prophet II software, to partner with them in setting up an initial pilot.

It was an ideal situation from the beginning. The team had everything needed to launch the pilot: executive support, experienced resources, and an appetite for change. Everyone involved in the project expressed the same desire—better process information—and all saw ABM as the answer. The team was comprised of two individuals from finance, with the remainder from operations. Three team members served as the core team and worked full-time on the project, while the rest concentrated part-time on their particular functional areas.

Launching the Pilot

The pilot served as the training vehicle through which Hoffmann-La Roche team members learned about the ABM process. The exercise focused on sterile manufacturing, a part of the company that makes relatively small-volume products for intravenous and ophthalmic use, all of which go through sterilization procedures. There were four functional areas involved: materials management, maintenance, sterile manufacturing, and quality control. The pilot was designed to highlight the ability of ABM to show end-to-end process costs across organizational boundaries (see Exhibit 5–1).

Quality control, for example, is that portion of the manufacturing process that provides critical testing and inspection of the products and their inputs. The group tests virtually everything involved in the process, from active ingre-

Exhibit 5-1

Process Flow Across Organizational Boundaries

Capital Purchases	Grounds Maint.	Prepare Vials	Test Environ.
Production Planning	Line Maint.	Fill Vials	Test Lot
Distribution Planning	Equipment Maint.	Visually Inspect	Test Raw Material

Materials Management — Maintenance — Sterile Manufacturing — Quality Control

■ = Processes covered in pilot

dients, product containers, and water to the plant environment.

Quality control, obviously, is an essential element of the pharmaceutical manufacturing process. The ABM pilot identified a number of key opportunities to help streamline the process.

Process Improvement

The data and information gathered for the ABM process helped generate a clearer understanding of the entire quality control operation and its costs. In the production area, ABM identified the high labor costs involved in some routine visual inspections. Many inspections could be performed more economically by automated means yet attain the same results. The ABM process helped show precisely how much the company was spending on each step, paving the way for streamlining processes without interfering with stringent quality standards.

Just-in-Time

Arthur Andersen introduced the Just-in-Time (JIT) training technique to the Hoffmann-La Roche team. Instead of teaching the implementation team members ABM methodology and processes in their entirety at the beginning of the project, the consultants conducted training classes in necessary processes immediately before the implementation team was ready to perform the particular phase (see Exhibit 5-2). The JIT approach more closely matches instruction to its practical application, making it far more effective.

Exhibit 5-2

Hoffmann-La Roche Activity-Based Management Training Schedule

	Responsibility	Completion Date
1000 Project Organization		
1100 Perform "ABM Introduction" Mini-Training		
1200 Finalize project calendar		
2000 Activity Analysis		
2100 Perform "Activity Analysis" Mini-Training		
2200 Schedule and conduct process focus groups		
2300 Prepare preliminary Activity Dictionary		
3000 Model Design		
3100 Perform "ABM Software Refresher Mini-Training"		
3200 Design preliminary model schematic		

For example, at the beginning of the activity analysis phase, the project manager explained concepts such as the activity dictionary, how activities would be defined, and the definition of drivers. Before the model design phase began, the project manager walked the members though procedures as they actually built a sample model on the software.

Although JIT training was meant to fully prepare the team to implement ABM processes, actual implementation of critical phases was never rushed. When it came time to develop the model schematic, the team took the process a little slower than it might have. "Keeping in mind the training aspect of the engagement, we allowed additional time for some of the more difficult aspects of model development. Instruction on activity organization, model design, and the basics of the software were all given additional attention," noted Arthur Andersen team member Dana Glorie.

All told, the team identified about 70 activities for 45 products from the four functional segments. Sterile production was the centerpiece of the model and the largest of the four functional areas included. Only those activities included in the other functional segments that directly supported sterile manufacturing were represented. Each functional subteam was ultimately responsible for designing and building its own segment of the model, ensuring as much hands-on model time as possible for all team members.

Change Management

Throughout the pilot process, Arthur Andersen spent considerable time working with the Hoffmann-La Roche team helping members absorb the various aspects of ABM. One of the softer concepts the team quickly began to recognize was the importance of change management and organizational acceptance of the initiative. Dwight Snyder, manager of ABM at Hoffmann-La Roche, notes: "ABM acceptance hinges on ownership of the model at the functional department manager level." The team continually focused on maintaining open communications with all functional personnel to help speed information gathering and quickly dispel rumors concerning "hidden project objectives."

A Successful Pilot

The pilot was officially completed, on schedule, eight weeks after it had begun. The results clearly showed the advantages of the ABM perspective of costs. Viewing costs from both the process and product dimension highlighted the power of ABM. However, simply viewing the costs was not the only objective of the pilot. Mr. Schmukler continually emphasized the importance of "exercising the models" and stressed to the team that the pilot would not be complete until opportunities for improvement were identified. The team responded by identifying some $2 million in immediate improvements that could be implemented by the end of the year. Responsibility for making the indicated changes was assigned immediately, and strict time lines were set (see Exhibit 5–3).

The project's steering committee chair, Chuck Flemming, vice president of Technical Operations, did not miss the accelerated payback of the pilot. Fleming noted that the concept of picking up savings as you go is an excellent approach for maintaining executive support.

Word of the pilot's success spread quickly throughout the organization. Project team members received numerous requests asking that they share what they had learned. The team was poised for full implementation.

The original project team then split into individual implementation teams to continue implementation. Each new functional team leader developed an implementation plan for his or her organization and ABM was now under way for the entire Nutley operation. A separate integration team was formed to automate data collection and model updates for the initiative. An ABM administrator position was created and filled to coordinate the rapidly expanding integration. The small pilot concentrated in sterile manufacturing has opened the way for Hoffmann-La Roche's much larger and more comprehensive ABM goals.

Exhibit 5–3

"Exercising the Model" Through Implementation

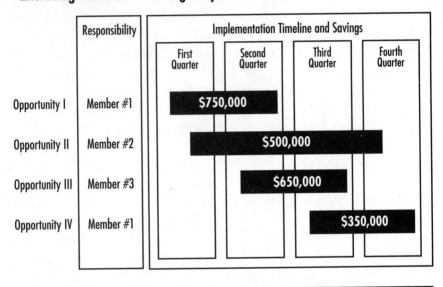

LESSONS LEARNED

- Have a dedicated champion who can obtain and maintain essential top management support.
- Set a clear direction from the outset and set firm scope boundaries to keep the team focused and minimize distracting details.
- Let the pilot be a learning experience for the team members. ABM is generally a new concept that must be well understood by the team.
- Don't try to address every detail in the pilot. As implementation team members become more comfortable with the methodology, they can more closely align their ABM models to their process.
- As a consultant (either internal or external), you are actually working yourself out of a job. Success is only achieved when the "client" no longer requires support.
- Just-in-Time training can be an effective way to match instruction to the training's practical application.

6

USING STORYBOARDING TO DEVELOP AN ABM SYSTEM

Johnson & Johnson Medical, Inc.
Arlington, Texas

MARK A. MOELLING

Mark A. Moelling is a Senior Manager with Arthur Andersen LLP in Dallas; he was formerly an employee of Johnson & Johnson Medical, Inc.

SUMMARY

Business Issues

Johnson & Johnson Medical, Inc. (JJMI) was facing competitive pressures on several fronts including declining market share and eroding margins. Traditionally, JJMI had successfully maintained costs by fostering continuous improvement programs in its plants. But JJMI recognized that it needed to go beyond its traditional cost maintenance programs to reduce costs and overhead expenses.

How ABM Was Used

JJMI's comprehensive ABM program focused on eliminating waste and increasing efficiency. Achieving management buy-in was a prerequisite.

Initially the team employed activity-based costing to improve the accuracy of reported product costs at JJMI's Arlington, Texas, manufacturing facility. However, the strategic costing approach was met with low acceptance. It did not yield significant improvements. Rather than abandon efforts completely, management switched focus from ABC to ABM.

The ABM methodology was applied to the areas of purchasing, sales, finance, information systems, manufacturing, and various segments of administration. Continued successes in cost reductions were demonstrated. These savings were used to finance the program. Steps were taken to ensure complete acceptance and integration into each employee's daily job, including reducing the number of steps to do the activity. For example, if it previously took 15 steps to pay a bill, the employee now processed the activity in 11 steps. When ABM proved successful, ABM was implemented companywide.

Johnson & Johnson's Results

As a result of ABM, JJMI was able to realize significant savings over a three-year period.

Johnson & Johnson Medical, Inc. (JJMI) is a wholly owned subsidiary of Johnson & Johnson, a Fortune 50 company that specializes in medical, pharmaceutical, and personal care products. JJMI is headquartered in Arlington, Texas and supplies health care providers with products such as surgical gloves, wound care products, vascular access products, anticlotting agents, and disinfecting agents. The company markets more than 1,500 different medical products under 76 brands. Hospitals are the prime customers. The products are manufactured in various locations, including Texas, Florida, and Puerto Rico, and in *maquiladora* plants along the U.S.–Mexican border.

The company needed to implement ABM because it was facing competitive pressures on several fronts, including declining market share and eroding margins. Previously, JJMI had successfully maintained costs by fostering continuous improvement programs in its plants, emphasizing responsiveness to customers' needs, which included supplier management and world-class manufacturing.

But JJMI needed to go beyond its traditional cost maintenance programs to reduce costs and overhead expenses. ABM was chosen as the means to accomplish that end. Ultimately, both ABC and ABM were implemented at JJMI to achieve these goals.

The Business Environment

JJMI's critical success factors include:

- quality (to be the leader in providing high-quality products and services);
- innovation (to provide a steady stream of new products and services);
- best value (to be the best cost producer of high-quality products); and
- total employee involvement (to provide an environment in which all associates could excel).

JJMI's cost accounting systems relied on traditional approaches to cost measurement and control. The systems did not take into account various cost drivers that affected the bottom line. For example, product costs were computed from direct costs (material and labor) plus a charge for overhead based on direct labor dollars. Each production cell had a different overhead rate.

Cost control was achieved by using detailed forecasts of expense items and computations of variance from standard. Forecasts and variances were computed for more than 8,000 expense items monthly.

How ABC and ABM Were Used

An internal ABM consulting group, organized to begin the ABC process, faced three hurdles. The group had to: obtain buy-in for the ABC program; find a way to finance the program; and determine how to cost products using ABC.

There were many challenges. Employees had little understanding of ABC and its value, which made buy-in difficult to obtain. To persuade management and to validate the program's value, it was necessary to pinpoint areas of waste not identified by traditional accounting systems. To finance the program, the ABC team identified various positions in the company's cost accounting department that were not required, reducing head count from four to one.

The ABC team used two different approaches to cost products: an interviewing circuit and storyboarding. During the interviewing circuit, the ABC team established cross-functional teams that included representatives from electronic data processing, material management, and operations. ABC team members interviewed the cross-functional teams one by one, asking questions about the work done in each department. The information was used to compile a chart of all activities and account for the costs related to those activities.

The interviewing process was not exemplary as a cost accounting measure and failed to produce significant results. It was very time consuming to get through all departments. The accuracy and detail obtained was not adequate. The managers interviewed did not know all the steps involved in their subordinates' jobs. Additionally, employees were nervous about handing over information. Compounding those problems, employees were nervous that their jobs would be eliminated if their specific responsibilities were deemed non-value-added (not contributing to the customer's needs).

At this point in the evolution of the initiative, the team attempted to bypass the obstacles that were plaguing the earlier trials. The ABC group decided to train the interviewers to interview more effectively. This wasn't of much help. Although much effort was put toward training, the interviewing progress was still slow. In short, failure resulted because management did not understand the approach and the program was viewed as a typical accounting project. Employees were getting lost in the details, making accurate counts of tasks and activities impossible. To remedy these problems, the group introduced activity-based management and storyboarding.

The primary objective of ABM was process improvement. Achieving that goal would require a shift in which employees would focus on problem solving, not costing, to achieve process improvement. The immediate goal of ABM was to obtain accurate data on processes; product costing was rescheduled for a later phase of the project. This shift in emphasis made all the difference.

"When we started the project, our objective was to obtain more accurate product costs," commented one ABM team member. "It was only later that we realized how many steps existed in the administrative processes. When we saw the picture being painted of the tasks that made up the daily jobs, *we found that we could get wows in the administrative areas, too*. Now that we are doing ABM, our objective is to improve first, and cost products second."

At the same time, storyboarding was selected as a data collection method in which the activities of a process are mapped visually (see Exhibit 6–1). The storyboarding technique allows participants to own the process of problem solving. The ABM team hoped that this approach would facilitate acceptance and buy-in. Storyboarding was implemented in all administrative departments: manufacturing, research and development, finance, marketing, sales, purchasing, and management information systems. Natural work teams of department managers and staff were formed. Team composition reflected how the various departments worked together on an everyday basis.

In order to make sure that storyboarding was implemented consistently

Exhibit 6-1

Storyboard Example Using Arthur Andersen's Rapid Vision© Board

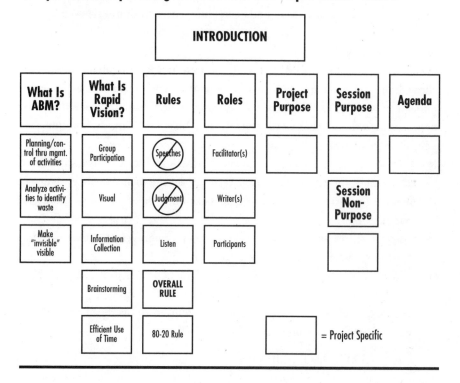

across all departments, a standardized process was developed. An internal ABM consulting team facilitator would meet with the work team for three to four hours in three separate sessions at one-week intervals. The facilitator provided ABM process guidance but left responsibility for developing output in the hands of the work team.

The objective of the first session was to introduce the work team to ABM, to identify activities and the time and resources they consume, and to pinpoint opportunities for improvement. In the second session, the team set performance metrics and identified the customers as well as the suppliers of each activity. In the third session, the team identified actions to be taken for process improvement: organized opportunities according to controllability; articulated causes of problems; assigned an owner to each problem; and set a date for its elimination.

The benefits of the new approach were obvious almost immediately: it was simple and participants owned the process, enabling them to view the program as a way of looking after their own interests. By using storyboarding, process turnaround time for results was shortened to two days rather than several weeks with the traditional approach. The quality of information it yielded was much more accurate than that which had been obtained through interviewing.

Results at JJMI

ABM was successful at JJMI not only because it came to broad acceptance throughout the company, but also because the ABM team was experienced enough to remain flexible in the face of early failures. Using the storyboarding approach was the critical factor that made JJMI's ABM implementation successful. Ultimately, ABM:

- contributed to the accomplishment of JJMI's financial goals and reduced cycle times for processes in new product development, finance, management information systems, the field sales force, sales administration, and purchasing;
- empowered the workforce to make necessary improvements that had dramatic effects on the company's bottom line;
- allowed employees to take ownership of the activities to accomplish both individual and department objectives; and
- encouraged employees to pay constant attention to overhead and to view waste elimination as an ongoing process.

Once ABM helped JJMI to identify and measure metrics for quality improvement, ABM was incorporated into JJMI's total quality improvement plan, contributing to a significant part of the quality improvement plan objectives companywide. As a result of its comprehensive ABM program that focused on eliminating waste and increasing efficiency, JJMI was able to realize significant savings over a three-year period.

LESSONS LEARNED

- Involving the employees who do the work through visual techniques such as storyboarding is a key to achieving companywide support.
- Maintaining the momentum of cost savings that were achieved early on is key to enjoying long-term success with ABM.
- Most administrative tasks may not appear to be systematic; therefore it can be difficult to identify processes.
- ABM needs to be cross-functional in its implementation in order to garner companywide support.

7

USING ABM TO SUPPORT REENGINEERING

Pennzoil Exploration & Production Company,
Houston, Texas

CRAIG R. COLLINS AND ANGELA A. MINAS

Craig R. Collins is an Experienced Manager with Arthur Andersen LLP in Dallas.
Angela A. Minas is a Senior Manager with Arthur Andersen LLP in Houston.

SUMMARY

Business Issues
To keep pace with lower crude oil and natural gas prices and slowing North American operations, the Pennzoil Production and Exploration Company (PEPCO) needed to find ways to increase value and/or reduce costs. To achieve these reductions, company executives sought to make strategic changes in the mix of oil and gas properties the company owned and operated. They also sought to reengineer existing processes to streamline and improve efficiency. A full-time reengineering team was created to analyze and develop a plan to achieve these objectives.

How ABM Was Used
Activity-based management was used as a key measurement tool to identify costs by process and to support the reengineering efforts. A joint Pennzoil/Arthur Andersen ABM team held focus group sessions and conducted quantitative and qualitative surveys among 1,700 PEPCO employees to determine what activities were being performed.

Using a custom database, the team developed a software model oriented to oil and gas operations that classifies Pennzoil properties and ranks them in terms of cost and effort required. Properties can now be assessed in terms of their fully loaded cost, including general and administrative support costs, which can be compared to the size and value of those properties to rank investments.

ABM analysis indicated areas with high improvement potential, which became the focus of reengineering task groups. A data management initiative resulted from the knowledge of how much was spent on data gathering and manipulation as opposed to value-added analysis.

The Results for Pennzoil
As a result of the ABM analysis, Pennzoil now knows and understands the operating and general and administrative (G&A) costs associated with producing properties and activities instead of having a G&A cost pool. The company used the ABM model to quantitatively support their reengineering and reorganization planning processes.

Oil and gas companies have always faced erratic swings in profitability. This is particularly true in the industry since 1986. To cope, many have turned to more advanced management tools to help ensure consistent profitability. Pennzoil sought to achieve this goal by using an ABM system to facilitate its reengineering of the exploration and production activities.

Pennzoil's Business Environment
Faced with a maturing world oil market, Pennzoil recognized the need to reduce operating and general and administrative (G&A) costs. This effort was focused at Pennzoil Exploration and Production Company's (PEPCO) North American operations. Before beginning an aggressive cost reduction program, the company needed a reliable analysis detailing which properties were profitable, which

were not, and precisely how much the $2-billion exploration and production company spent on each of its activities.

PEPCO organized a reengineering team of committed employees from all divisions and dedicated them full-time to the project. Arthur Andersen helped develop a special ABM model that could be adapted to support PEPCO's process improvement efforts.

The ABM Program

Arthur Andersen's plan defined four target benefits from ABM:

- perform cost reductions based on asset opportunity costs;
- identify opportunities to reduce costs by reengineering processes and managing cost drivers;
- establish a system that realistically assesses the benefits of reengineering; and
- provide a foundation for an ongoing performance measurement system and benchmarking framework.

The PEPCO/Arthur Andersen team began by creating a comprehensive activity dictionary, which classified activities performed by personnel into numerous categories (see Exhibit 7–1 for examples of the categories).

Exhibit 7–1

Activity Category Classifications

acquisitions	human resources planning
divestitures	revenue processing
well engineering	joint interest management
reservoir surveillance	reserves management
drilling	Securities and Exchange Commission (SEC) reporting
field operations	general accounting
construction	land and lease records
transportation	

The team organized focus group sessions for some 1,700 PEPCO employees at various company locations in Texas, Louisiana, Mississippi, Utah, Pennsylvania, and Canada. They asked each participant to complete a two-part survey dealing with the nature of his or her work (see Exhibit 7–2).

The survey provided the reengineering team with specific information about each PEPCO activity. Operations personnel also indicated whether the tasks were critical and how frequently they were performed.

Exhibit 7-2

Labor Information and Activity Effort Surveys

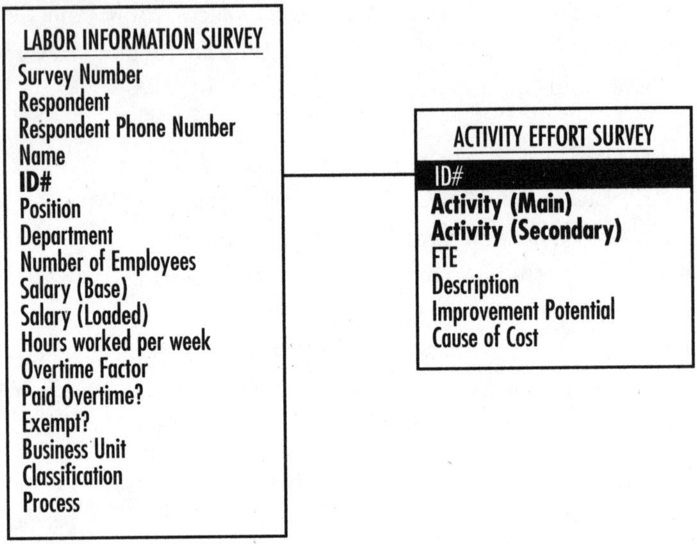

```
LABOR INFORMATION SURVEY
Survey Number
Respondent
Respondent Phone Number                  ACTIVITY EFFORT SURVEY
Name
ID#                                      ID#
Position                                 Activity (Main)
Department                               Activity (Secondary)
Number of Employees                      FTE
Salary (Base)                            Description
Salary (Loaded)                          Improvement Potential
Hours worked per week                    Cause of Cost
Overtime Factor
Paid Overtime?
Exempt?
Business Unit
Classification
Process
```

"This project will help us take a new look at our fundamental business processes and the activities that cause the company to incur costs," states the survey's prologue. "It will expose where we have problems and inefficiencies that cause anxiety and frustration, and it will help us make Pennzoil a better company."

Quantitative and Qualitative Questions

The survey's quantitative questions related to individual activities and the degree of effort expended by employees performing them. The survey also included introspective qualitative inquiries such as:

- What suggestions do you have for improving the work processes to reduce exceptions/rework outside your group's control?
- Suppose that one year from now you were describing the results of having successfully implemented significant improvements to your work processes. What would you have accomplished?
- If it were within your power, what change would you make to improve overall company performance?

Employees had many opportunities to make recommendations and to question tasks they believed didn't make sense or could be done better. Their comments were eventually linked to specific processes.

Custom-Designed Database

The surveys generated hundreds of detailed responses, which were fed into a Microsoft Access database custom designed for the ABM project. The project team tailored the software to the oil and gas industry, enabling team members to analyze PEPCO's 500-plus activities and track costs associated with processes, activities, and properties (see Exhibits 7–3 and 7–4 for an overview of the flow of general and administrative costs).

The customized software also allowed for analysis of activities by user-defined characteristics (also called attribute analysis), assignment of activities to specific PEPCO properties, and "what if" scenario modeling. In addition, the computer model presented detailed costs associated with each activity at each property, thereby allowing Pennzoil to drill down into the data to determine the source of incurred costs.

The customized database was also used to capture unique characteristics for each property. For instance, the data showed the number of joint-interest owners associated with each field, the number of royalty owners, and the number of producing wells. In addition to allowing properties to be profiled, this data can be used to evaluate what changes in activities result from the sale or acquisition of a property.

The team could also compare total revenue and costs of operating a property with perceived values of reserves to determine the strategic value of selling certain properties. These analyses were used in conjunction with PEPCO's comprehensive inventory of its assets. Geological studies previously grouped assets in categories using names like "jewels," "high values," "mid-values," and "exotics." The ABC analysis coordinated the G&A costs associated with producing properties to enable investment comparisons on a more meaningful basis.

To further facilitate the reengineering efforts, the custom ABM data provides linkage and support for a number of analysis tools (see Exhibit 7–5 for an overview).

Typical quality improvement tools such as pareto analysis and "5 Whys" analysis were used as was the Global Best Practices Knowledge Base[SM] from Arthur Andersen. Activity-specific analysis included driver, secondary activity, and several types of activity characteristics such as whether the activity is manually or systems intensive, or creative versus repetitive. The team also reviewed

Exhibit 7–3

Activity-Based General and Administrative Cost Flow

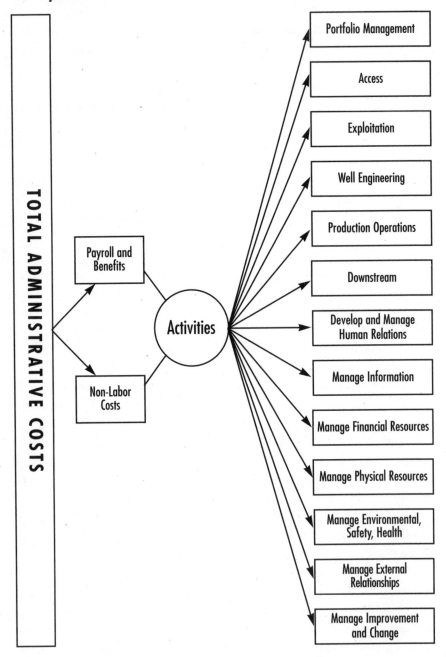

Exhibit 7-4

Activity-Based General and Administrative Cost Flow

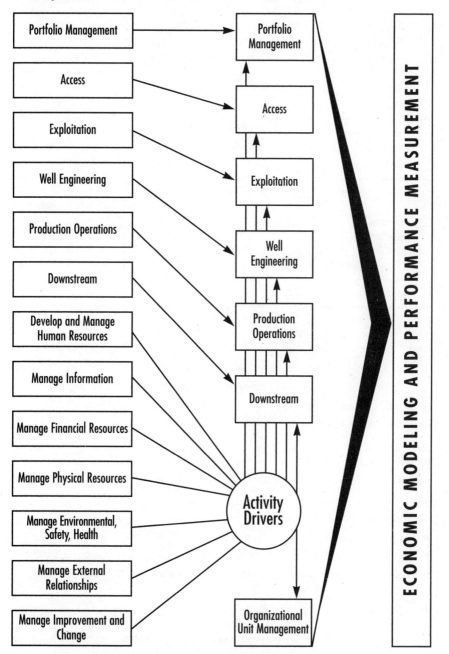

Exhibit 7-5

Activity Analysis to Support Reengineering

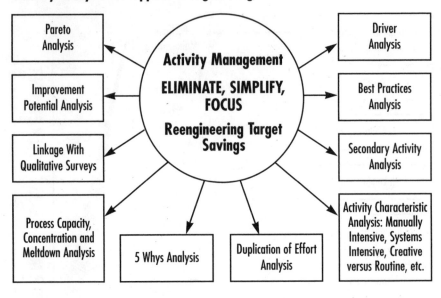

for duplication of efforts, linked activities with the qualitative surveys and evaluated process capacity to identify concentration and meltdown points.

All of these analyses lead to analysis and identification of improvement potential. By seeking to first eliminate activities, simply those that remain, and focus the streamlined efforts, PEPCO set significant reengineering targets.

Results of the Model

All told, the ABM model provided many new opportunities that PEPCO could now use to:

- build production and administrative cost models;
- model fixed and variable cost components of each process;
- determine the impact of divestitures on operating and administrative costs;
- model the resource requirements associated with reorganizational changes; and
- establish process benchmarks and performance measures.

In addition, PEPCO developed an economic model for assigning costs to all of its properties. By understanding each property's economic value on a fully costed basis, management could use this model to help determine which properties to retain and which to sell.

After seeing the benefits derived from the ABM data, PEPCO management expanded the use of the model to assist in a companywide reorganization encompassing regrouping assets, prioritizing properties, creating or eliminating internal organizations, and accurately determining which activities and resources were essential to profitability. The ABM model played a major role in the reorganization by helping to determine resources required by the organization to support the assets.

Activity-based management provided the data for Pennzoil to change the cost structure of its exploration and production efforts. It achieved this by determining what resources were actually required to support their properties based on current operations. In addition, the reengineering link enabled the company to consider those same properties and determine how they could best meet their economic objectives with fewer resources through a variety of operations improvement analyses.

LESSONS LEARNED

- Integrating a well-blended reengineering team of professional and experienced employees with an ABM team can facilitate data collection as well as education of employees and management about the project and the changes it fosters.
- ABM is an effective model for planning company reorganization because it is a data gathering analytical tool and targeting device that helps a company more clearly understand its own objectives.
- Activity analysis provides a robust set of tools to understand and know how to reengineer business processes.

8

CONTINUOUS IMPLEMENTATION YIELDS DEEPER RESULTS

Current, Inc.
Colorado Springs, Colorado

ROBERT C. THAMES AND JOSEPH W. BAGAN

*Robert C. Thames and Joseph W. Bagan are
Senior Managers with Arthur Andersen LLP in Denver.*

SUMMARY

Business Issues

Current Inc.'s ABC process incorporates an ongoing, long-term system that is helping this $300-million-a-year firm track 3,500 unique products, assign profit margins to each one, and ensure that every item in its many catalogs pays for itself. Current was confronting increasing competition, declining profit margins, and a top management focus on bottom line results. Due to the high diversity of Current's product lines and the low dollar cost of those products, Current needed a way to better understand and manage both manufacturing and nonmanufacturing sources of product related cost.

How ABC Was Used

The primary purpose of ABC at Current was fundamental: to provide better information for decision making. The goal was to reflect manufacturing costs more accurately by identifying product characteristics that cause activities and costs to be incurred. Current was also interested in making product cost more inclusive through examination and aggregation of all costs required to create and deliver the product and service to the customer.

Current first began using ABC in 1991 as part of a pilot program in its primary manufacturing facility in Colorado Springs, Colorado. From the pilot, management then expanded ABC's use by implementing the system in phases with the eventual goal of a companywide, ongoing operation. Some of the project highlights include: identification of 600 major activities and 200 activity drivers covering 140 work centers; participation of the creative department composed of writers, designers, and illustrators whose activities are not as readily quantifiable as those in other departments; and more realistic apportionment of overhead costs among high- and low-volume products.

Current's Results

Success of the ABC program at Current is defined as the skillful use of the information ABC produces to support decision making. One key factor to the success and longevity of Current's ABC program can be found in the facilitative attitude of the members of the cost management team.

In addition, the group's continuing "sell" program for keeping new and existing executive and middle management up to date on the system's benefits and its importance to the company has contributed to its stability.

When you open the mailbox to a ubiquitous array of catalogs and direct-mail literature, it's hard to imagine that these colorful mailers represent one of the United States' largest and most meticulously maintained industries. You see only samplings of the huge volumes of printed materials, while someone somewhere is keeping tabs on every item.

Current, Inc., located in Colorado Springs, Colorado, has been printing and marketing paper goods such as greeting cards, calendars, educational materials, bank checks, and the like for 45 years. Operating as a division of Deluxe Printing since 1987, the company produces more than a dozen direct-mail promotional campaigns a year with catalogs that offer more than 3,500 products. This high-ly seasonal business redesigns some 75 percent of its product line each year to generate sales in excess of $300 million. New product introduction is a require-ment in the social expressions industry with constant changeover of items.

Company Culture

From a financial reporting perspective, Current had always required its depart-ments to allocate costs to specific business ventures. Thus it was not a major philosophical leap to introduce the concept of ABC into the organization. From the beginning, ABC was positioned as a tool for decision making, rather than the latest innovation in cost management (see Exhibit 8–1).

Exhibit 8–1

The Primary Benefits of Activity-Based Costing Are ...

- Determining more accurate product cost;
- Understanding activities that drive/cause costs;
- Linking decisions to subsequent costs (cause/effect/benefit relationships);
- Identifying improvement opportunities;
- "What if" analysis in the planning stage;
- Profit analysis by SKU, category, book, season ...

... better information for decision making.

According to a Current spokesperson, no one likes a member of the finance organization classifying activities as non-value-added. So Current managers use ABC to illuminate the savings opportunity for process improvements, while leaving the responsibility for making those improvements with its users. Current's internal training overview states: "ABC is a tool, not a club; a means, not an end."

Stock-Keeping Units

Current identifies each of its products by the familiar manufacturing term "stock-keeping unit" (generally known by its acronym, SKU, and pronounced "skew"). In 1991, Current was having difficulties with overallocation to promotional cam-paigns. Management concluded it was necessary to get a more precise focus on the cost of each product in the company's catalogs and to define how much prof-it was being generated by each SKU. The company wanted to know the total cost of each direct-mail campaign and the break-even profit margin generated per catalog in order to deem it a successful campaign. Considering Current's 3,500 SKUs and the high level of new product introductions, these were not easy tasks.

Working with a team of Arthur Andersen consultants, Current initiated a three month ABC pilot at its primary manufacturing facility, the Stone Street plant. What started out as a simple spreadsheet program turned into a pioneering example of target costing designed to help the company understand its product costs at the SKU level.

With the large number of products at widely varying margins, a change in the sales mix can result in dramatic margin savings. In new product development, ABC information allowed Current to understand which products to launch and which to discontinue. For example, ABC analysis allows everyone to understand the implications of batch sizes on production and stocking costs. In merchandising planning functions, where once there was a lack of cost ownership, demand for product contribution margin information has emerged as each product now must pay for itself.

The Road to a Long-Term Program

Initially, the benefits of the new costing system were uncertain. To convince Current's management of the need to incorporate an ABC system, Current's cost management group started its pilot in one of the most demanding sections of its printing department: the press room, which fills its Stone Street plant. When the pilot proved to be a success, the group set up a second pilot in packaging and personalization (i.e., customized orders such as monogrammed stationery), and later implemented pilots in the creative design, purchasing, and quality assurance departments (see Exhibit 8–2).

Exhibit 8-2

ABC at Current Benefited From a Phased Roll Out ...

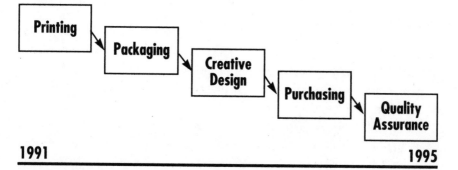

1991   1995

As the ABC initiative expanded through each phased step, the cost management group conducted extensive activity interviews and business process mapping. The creative department, which consists of writers, designers, and illustrators, was not as quantifiable as other groups, but its functions were important parts of the activity data. To ensure proper inclusion, the ABC team took each job description and job title through the interview process and had each individual describe his or her function. All told, Current identified more than 600 major activities and 200 activity drivers. (Current defines a major activity as one that requires more than five percent of an individual's time.) Through this detailed analysis, the team was able to provide much greater insight into how creative design impacted profitability.

Today, Current's ABC program has proved to be successful as an ongoing long-term program, and its end is nowhere in sight. The company has realized impressive improvements in profit margins, which was the primary goal of the program. In addition, the program's secondary objective was to attain significant manufacturing cost savings in terms of process improvements, reduced waste, and spoilage. The latter objective has achieved some initial savings and continues on an ongoing basis.

Custom-Designed Software

Because of the volume and rapid turnover of Current's product lines, the company's information systems employees, in conjunction with a contract programmer, designed all of Current's ABC software. It is still in use today.

By breaking down costs to the activity level, Current can obtain far more definable allocations of its overhead costs than was ever before possible. Compare, for example, a high-volume product, such as a popular Mother's Day greeting card, which may have a 100,000-copy press run, with a low-volume (2,000–3,000 copies), not-so-popular card. Traditionally, the company allocated overhead in terms of machine hours and labor costs; therefore, the high-volume product would absorb more of those costs.

ABC, however, identifies the activities that underpin these products and makes more accurate allocations of costs possible. Users are now very aware of the cost drivers in their operations and are taking appropriate action. ABC is the catalyst that shows the major swings between what a company thinks a product should cost and what it really does cost.

Current's ABC program is now an ongoing process. Specific areas of the company, including manufacturing, packaging, personalization, creative, and purchasing, are supported by the system. The company provides information from its ABC program as required by users, whether daily, weekly, or monthly. While the ABC model is updated annually as part of Current's new budget cycle, activities are continually cycled to keep up to date with corporate changes in operations. For example, if a new press or operational process is added, the model is updated immediately.

Summary and detail reports are designed to be user friendly and compare subcomponent costs in five areas: raw materials, one-time costs, direct costs, semitraceable, and nontraceable costs (see Exhibit 8–3).

Exhibit 8–3
Bill of Cost Detail

■ Raw Materials

■ Direct-Trace Costs: allocated directly to products
  – actual labor costs
  – actual machine operating costs
  – paid breaks

■ Semitrace Costs: assigned by activity
  – machine maintenance
  – production-related training
  – setup/cleanup of work areas
  – supervisor salaries

■ Nontrace Costs: small-pool allocation
  – building maintenance and insurance
  – building operating expenses

■ One-Time Costs

Project team members are beginning to move out into functional areas to cross-pollinate the cost management understanding. Departments are starting to perform more "make versus buy" decisions. Future plans call for attaching vendor-related costs such as acquisition costs, cost of quality, cost of customer dissatisfaction, cost of defective materials from vendors, cost of delays in receiving materials, etc. to the costs of Current's products.

Current's Critical Success Factors

Based on its experiences implementing its ABC program, Current cites a number of critical success factors including:

- Begin the program by building consensus on all levels of the organization, especially with management, and demonstrate the benefits up front. Show employees that ABC will not add to their already busy workload.

- Approach people in a nonthreatening way; precede requests with phrases like, "We are trying to get this information to provide the tools you need to enable you to do your job better."

- Anticipate resistance to change, especially when the company already has a standard costing system. Employees might question why a different one is needed.

- Make sure the ABC staffing fits the culture of the organization and that staffers portray themselves as problem solvers.

- Work as a cross-functional team. Solicit input and feedback. Explain concepts in the words employees would use, not in "accountantese." Show how a particular screen looks, how the information is highlighted.

- Set realistic goals. Know your resources and your resource constraints.

- Have baseline costs in hand before launching initiatives so you can later compare the improvements with original costs. Demonstrate quantitatively the value ABC has brought to operations.

- Review the processes and the costs with the internal experts and build data validity checks into the system.

- Make sure numbers and other critical information you use are correct before you publish them. Only well-trained users should have access to modifying the data. Projected cost figures should be able to be validated.

- Review any conclusions you reach with your team before making recommendations to senior management.

- Make sure information is easy to use and understand. It is important to solidify specific user inputs, how the screen should look, how the information should be highlighted.

- Demonstrate to users the types of benefits to be realized such as how jobs will be made easier or profit sharing will be improved.

- Keep pace with turnover in executive and middle management by continually selling the value of ABC, and educate new employees about its concepts.

LESSONS LEARNED

- ABC is a tool, not a club; a means, not an end.
- One of the greatest benefits ABC offers users is an opportunity to conduct "what if" exercises.
- Low-margin products may represent large-volume items in certain markets, and an extra point or two in cost saving can mean large dollar amounts in profit.
- Each product, no matter how small or inexpensive, can be made to pay for itself.
- Because of the relatively high turnover of management personnel in some companies, it is important to continue educating and selling the value of ABC and ABM to both new and existing managers.

9

MULTIPLE PROJECT ROLL-OUT CREATES LEVERAGE

The Marmon Group
Chicago, Illinois

John Vale

John Vale is a Senior Manager with Arthur Andersen LLP in Dallas.

SUMMARY

Business Issues

Senior executives at The Marmon Group of companies, a $5-billion conglomerate of more than 65 autonomous manufacturing and service companies worldwide, had long recognized that general managers often lacked an accurate understanding of the financial results of their decisions. Management decisions were based on solid operating principles, yet the anticipated financial benefits would not appear, at least not in the product lines in which they were expected. Based on these experiences, some operating managers virtually ignored their financial statements and, unfortunately, sometimes their financial managers as well.

The advent of activity-based management created the opportunity for The Marmon Group to introduce common sense operational cost accounting to its member companies. Conglomerate managers aggressively encouraged activity-based management and launched ABM programs in more than 30 Marmon companies within two years of introducing the concept.

Most Marmon companies already perform above their respective industry norms. ABM is geared toward ensuring continued growth and proper strategic focus.

How ABM Is Used

In two years ABM has become the management style at many Marmon member companies.
- Capital requests are tested through ABM models;
- Product or customer rationalization occurs via scenario playing;
- Negotiations are based on model results; and
- Efforts to control costs and change price structures are guided by activity costs.

Much of the advantage ABM delivers comes from managers who "live" ABM, sometimes using only very simple, low-cost models. All Marmon companies now produce ABM plans focused on net profit by product line or customer group.

The Results for Marmon

The Marmon Group has implemented ABM at 30 of its affiliated companies and continues to expand ABM to other affiliates.

In 1953, the Pritzker family acquired its first company in what eventually became The Marmon Group. Mr. R. A. Pritzker, president of The Marmon Group, embarked on a strategy to acquire a wide range of companies that would represent the automotive, energy, water treatment, credit reporting, mining, building products, distribution, and other industries. Marmon, headquartered in Chicago, is a $5-billion association of more than 65 manufacturing and services companies operating worldwide.

For the past 15 years, Marmon has consistently outperformed the Fortune 500 averages. Managers continuously strive for better ways to understand and operate their businesses.

An engineer by training, Pritzker firmly believes that proper cost accounting is vital to the long-term success of any company. Using what he calls common sense accounting, Pritzker constantly stresses the importance of understanding what it costs to make, sell, service, and administer products or services. He says, "This new activity-based accounting is the only adequate way to know what is really going on. Other financial statements are so complex only the accountants can understand them, and sometimes, I'm not sure *they* can."

Introducing ABM

As early as the 1950s, Pritzker developed costed activity charts for his manufacturing operations as well as administrative tasks, essentially pioneering an early version of ABC. It wasn't until the late 1980s that the accounting profession endorsed these early engineering concepts by introducing ABC.

In 1992, Jim Smith joined The Marmon Group and became the hub of the company's efforts to spread the use of activity-based concepts throughout the organization. Using previous ABM experience and selling the concepts internally, he has been able to start initiatives in more than 30 Marmon companies in the past three years.

Some of the early reactions at Marmon member companies have altered the ongoing programs. "We make a distinction between ABC and ABM," says Smith. "In fact, most companies changed the name to ABM so it wouldn't be interpreted as simply another cost accounting exercise. The term 'ABM' better represents the multifunctional use of the concept."

It is Smith's job to teach ABM to member company project teams and show how each company management group can benefit. Each general manager determines if, when, and how ABM will be started. As each company's managers must weigh the cost/benefit and other management initiatives, this localized decision-making process is time consuming; yet once buy-in is achieved, the approach assures management use of the results.

At Marmon, ABM is used only for valid management decision making purposes. "Companies that implement ABC as the latest and greatest system are doomed to fail," says Smith. Marmon boasts an 85 percent success rate in ABM acceptance because the results are important and are used.

According to Smith, there are two valid ways to use financial information for decision making and one invalid way. The two valid ways include ignoring it or using it. If the answers are obvious or if the decision is essential for nonfinancial reasons, cost information can and likely should be ignored. On the other hand, if a financial analysis is needed, the only way to do the job right is to use

ABM, even if only on a macro level to understand, for example, the proper allocation of overhead to products or services.

The invalid way to use financial information is the method generally used: the traditional cost system. Most operating managers agree the existing cost system smears overheads and incorrectly allocates costs of shipping, selling, engineering, and administration. Even though up to or more than 50 percent of a company's costs are incorrectly smeared, managers still use traditional cost reports to run their businesses (see Exhibit 9–1).

Exhibit 9–1

Traditonal Cost Allocations

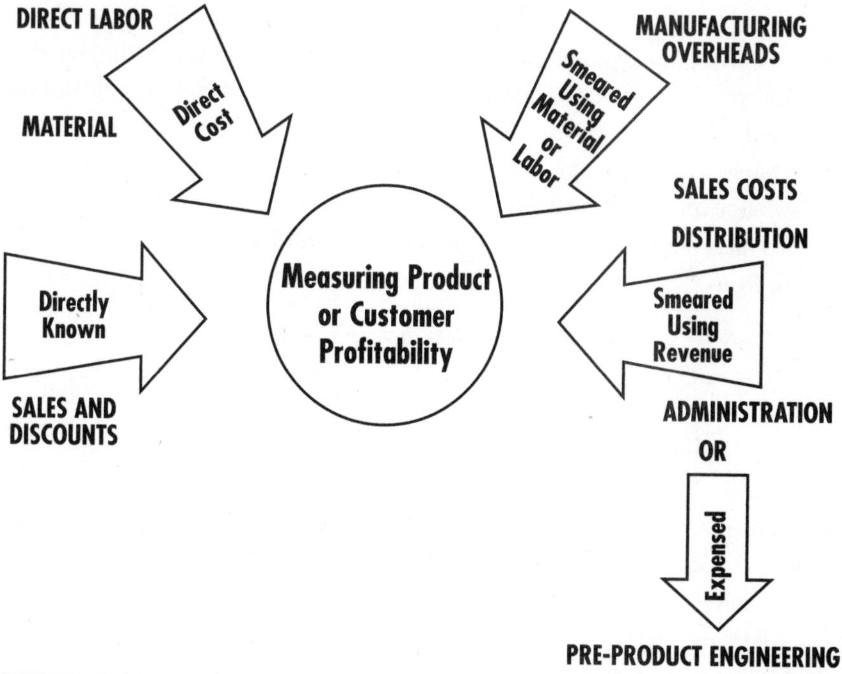

DIRECT LABOR

MATERIAL

Direct Cost

MANUFACTURING OVERHEADS

Smeared Using Material or Labor

SALES COSTS

DISTRIBUTION

Measuring Product or Customer Profitability

Directly Known

Smeared Using Revenue

SALES AND DISCOUNTS

ADMINISTRATION OR

Expensed

PRE-PRODUCT ENGINEERING

Roll-Out Strategy

Its structure as a "confederation" of autonomous companies enabled Marmon to use a particular technique known for achieving success: the roll-out strategy. Using The Model Approach developed by Sapling Corporation, ABM programs have been well accepted in most Marmon companies. The Marmon Group has stressed four essential tasks of a successful launch:

- Set a management objective for the business issue.
- Use a multifunctional internal team.
- Complete the entire project within 14 weeks.
- Communicate the results.

Management Objectives

Implementing ABM into an existing accounting system doesn't work. Instead, each Marmon company adopting ABM sets one or two major objectives for its first and follow-up ABM programs. These objectives are aimed at business issues that the company must address. Often, Smith advises member companies that don't have a business issue to wait for one. "Implementing ABM to keep the group office happy is likely a waste of everyone's time," he says. Examples of valid objectives in Marmon companies have included:

- Should we be in the gear-grinding business for locomotives?
- Are we correctly pricing services to our specialty banking customers?
- Is premium, customized mining equipment more or less profitable than standard, lower-priced versions?
- Do we require a major price increase to our leading customer? If required, what activity costs will help justify the increase?
- To meet a target price for our new product, on which activities do we need to focus?

These are questions that interest managers. When ABM answers these questions and provides supporting detail, managers become believers. An objective such as getting training in ABC may be valid, but it doesn't generate the interest that broader, more strategic objectives like those listed above can create.

Arthur Andersen's Chuck Marx agrees with the Marmon approach: "It's impressive that Marmon encourages each member company to focus on the results it wants to achieve with ABM and to launch quite different projects to achieve those results."

Marmon's experience at Trans Union Corporation illustrates how results from ABM projects that address specific objectives can be used. This supplier of credit reporting information knew it had some pricing concerns in a portion of its business. The company planned to implement a price change without a specific financial analysis when ABM was introduced. After several weeks, managers had a great deal more information on which prices needed changing and which could remain unchanged. The division vice president said, "Without ABM we'd still be underpricing by tens of thousands of dollars."

Fourteen-Week Time Limits

One of the impediments to setting an objective for an ABM project is the waiting period between project conceptualization and results. Management usually wants to make a decision within a week or two of setting the objective, but it takes six to fourteen weeks to complete an ABM project. Consequently, the objective for an initial ABM project must be one that can wait for the project to be completed.

Because Marmon places an overriding emphasis on use of ABM project results, certain criteria to ensure the results' utility have been set: projects must obtain results within 14 weeks and objectives must be sufficiently long-term so that waiting for the project to be completed does not defeat the purpose of the project (see Exhibit 9–2 for a typical 14-week project plan).

Exhibit 9–2

Typical Marmon Project

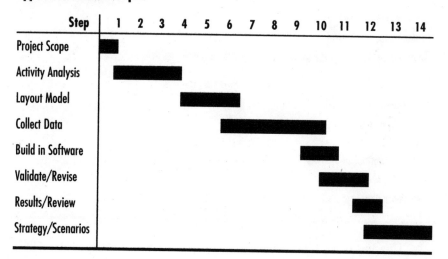

In some cases, however, project teams will pull out all the stops to complete a project. For example, Fontaine Fifth Wheel, a Marmon company that manufactures hitches that connect 18-wheel tractor trailers to trucks, had only a few weeks in which to evaluate an opportunity to change product mix at two existing plants and build a third plant to meet expanded customer demand. After considering its options, Fontaine chose to launch an ABM project rather than undertake a non-ABM-related financial analysis.

Fontaine put together a team consisting of five primary members: an operations manager, an industrial engineer, an information systems manager, a cost accountant, and an Arthur Andersen facilitator. Working 16 hours a day for six days a week, the team successfully developed not only an analysis of the opportunity but several "what if" scenarios to prove what was and was not possible from the planned change. It also successfully broke the Marmon ABM project completion record: the team finished its work in only four weeks. The models have since justified the capital expansion and the efficiency improvements. Currently, a multimillion-dollar profit enhancement project is underway at the company.

Multifunctional Teams

Another technique contributing to Marmon's success has been the use of multifunctional teams. Obtaining a variety of input is critical for a valid ABM model. Project teams range in size from two to eight people with core members moving on to additional projects as needed (see Exhibit 9–3 for a sample team profile).

Exhibit 9–3

Sample of Multifunctional Team Composition

Member	Time Commitments
Project Leader	80%
Operations Manager	15%
Industrial Engineer	15%
Manager, Information Systems	30%
Financial Analyst	30%
Sales/Marketing	15%

The single most important team member is the project leader. Smith believes that this individual accounts for more than 70 percent of the reason for a particular company's success or failure. He says, "Some managers I speak to find the reasons why what they are doing is okay, others constantly search for reasons to change what they are doing. When I find one of these change agents, I have no worries about a successful launch."

The change agents can come from any profession. Marmon has enjoyed great success with industrial engineers, operating management, quality managers, information systems, and cost accounting serving as leaders. Although financial managers have an uphill battle to be accepted as change agents, their plight is not insurmountable. However, if a finance staff member is labeled as being out of touch with operations, too theoretical, stuck in analysis paralysis, or noncommunicative, another project leader who will be supported by finance is a better choice.

ABM training is also critical to successful implementations. At Wells Lamont, one of the world's leading glove manufacturers, training in the ABM concept has been one of the biggest factors of success. This $200-million company has sent more than 60 managers and staff for ABM training. In the past two years, Wells Lamont has had 15 project members conducting more than seven projects, with an extra five to six new projects per year in the planning stage.

What does Wells Lamont gain by so much involvement? Lloyd Rogers, the company's president, says, "The concepts of ABM are a further refinement of where we were headed in managing our business. A few years ago, I introduced customer and product reporting that focused on net income and highlighted the differences between variable and fixed costs. ABM is the system to spread this concept throughout the company. It's not just a financial system, it can be understood and supported by all employees from any profession and from any level of management."

Training also offers a major benefit when employees view the ABM concept simply as a management principle. After taking the basic ABM training seminar, a sales manager at a Marmon mining equipment company commented, "This course should be required for all sales people. It shows the numbers so non-financial types can follow them."

Communicate Results

Multisite, multicompany organizations like The Marmon Group require one other critical success factor. Good results in one area or company have to be communicated to other areas or companies in order to generate interest.

At Marmon's headquarters, Smith acts as a bulletin board as well as a trainer and facilitator. He says, "Nothing gains acceptance for ABM better than a success story that you can relate to." At Marmon, the success story may derive from a sister company's ABM program or a valuable lesson discovered within a division of the same company. As Smith travels to various Marmon companies, he spreads word of recent ABM successes, carefully choosing examples that other managers can understand.

Smith also speaks of the conglomerate's member company initiatives at organized group functions. However, he noticed that the flurry of renewed interest in ABM that was generated following a group function trailed off after a few weeks. The insight led to the launch of *The Marmon Cost Manager*, a quarterly newsletter that puts member company successes—whether small changes or million-dollar findings—on view and offers advice on problems common to Marmon companies. *The Marmon Cost Manager* is sent to almost a thousand Marmon employees at all levels.

The newsletter also answers a question posed by many Marmon managers, most of whom now agree that ABM information is valuable: "Is it available at a reasonable cost?" Each issue of *The Marmon Cost Manager* illustrates how a project staffed by local employees, lasting 14 weeks, and costing a few thousand dollars can provide valuable insight that doesn't require a major payback.

The Marmon Group's Results

Since many Marmon projects do not lead to dramatic immediate change, judging success can be difficult. Yet, finding out that your largest customer is not a profitable one is important, even if action to change the situation cannot be taken immediately. Identifying cost reduction opportunities that can be held in reserve and introduced during the next business downturn can yield an impressive upswing in company market share when competitors are struggling.

Marmon Group President R. A. Pritzker nonetheless believes in the success of ABM. "ABM has done more in the past two years for our companies' understanding their costs than I have been able to achieve in the last 40 years," he says.

LESSONS LEARNED

- Traditional cost systems smear many overhead costs improperly and ignore others altogether while ABM closely traces all costs to their cost objects.
- Process modeling allows operating executives to understand and effectively manage their businesses. It turns ABC into ABM.
- Link your ABM implementation to solving one or two clear business issues. It will dramatically improve the interest level and lower the resistance to change. If you currently do not have a business issue, wait to implement ABM until you do.
- In a large company, successful roll-out of ABM requires management focus on the use of results rather than imposition of a new system. By requiring results in 14 weeks, the team focuses on adding value from the implementation.
- Effective implementation should be communicated constantly. This reenforces buy-in from other units.

IO

USING ABC FOR PROCESS ANALYSIS, CUSTOMER PROFITABILITY, AND MANUFACTURING FLEXIBILITY

Bliss & Laughlin Industries, Inc.
Harvey, Illinois

CHUCK MARX WITH JASON BALOGH

Chuck Marx is a Partner with Arthur Andersen LLP in Chicago.
Jason Balogh is a Senior Consultant with Arthur Andersen LLP in Chicago.

SUMMARY

Business Issues

With sales increasing and earnings declining, Bliss & Laughlin Industries, Inc. (B&L), a steel-finishing firm, needed to make the necessary strategic and operational changes to improve its long-term profitability.

B&L has an extensive product offering of approximately 800 standard steel products plus many items produced to customer specifications. The products are used primarily by original equipment manufacturers, automotive companies, and service centers.

How ABC Was Used

B&L turned to ABC to help quantify problem areas and identify opportunities for improvement. ABC helped the company focus on its main sources of income by revealing that 80 percent of its sales come from 10 percent of its customers and 20 percent of its product categories. ABC provided visibility to eight cross-functional business processes, which helped determine where operating costs could be consolidated or eliminated. ABC at B&L includes a profit planning process for both products and customers.

The Results for B&L

One year after implementing ABC, B&L had achieved substantial reductions in production costs, implemented plant improvements, and improved customer profitability resulting in more than $2 million in improved earnings. By using a benchmarking process across all of its plants, B&L identified significant additional long-term cost reduction opportunities.

The challenges of the 1990s came swiftly for Bliss & Laughlin Industries, Inc. (B&L), a 100-year-old steel company based in Harvey, Illinois. In 1988, the year the company went public, sales and earnings reached record highs. For the next four years, even as the company's sales continued to rise, earnings declined dramatically. Management reversed this trend by renewing its focus on profitable growth. Within one year, B&L regained its niche as one of the leading cold drawing steel mills in North America.

The route the company used to regain its strength was an activity-based costing analysis to generate a new strategic view of costs, including its customers, products, and manufacturing processes. During the period from 1988 to 1991, the company went from generating net earnings of more than $2 million to losing more than $3.6 million. In 1994, however, with the help of ABC, B&L earned $3.6 million (see Exhibit 10–1).

Implementing ABC

In 1992, after several tough years of operating losses, Greg Parker, the chairman, president, and CEO of B&L, asked Arthur Andersen to direct the implementa-

Exhibit 10-1

Net Earnings Compared
(amounts in thousands)

	1991		1994	
Net Sales	$114,528		$152,435	
Cost of Sales	(107,545)		(136,173)	
Gross Profit	6,983	(6%)	16,262	(11%)
Selling/Administrative/Interest	(10,645)	(9%)	(12,631)	(8%)
Pretax Income (Loss)	$ (3,662)		$ 3,631	

Source: 1994 Annual Report

---

tion of an ABC system to determine where the company's problems and opportunities lie. B&L's top management team took part in every phase of the study and participated in regular ABC staff meetings. The team was able to test many decisions against the ABC model, Net Prophet II, produced by Sapling Corporation of Toronto. This model allowed the project team to assist top management by testing the potential impact of their business decisions. The model also helped predict future cost savings.

Instead of creating a budgeting environment based on costs, the Arthur Andersen ABC team suggested a system of planning for profits. The profit planning formula uses the assumption that price minus required profits equals maximum produced and delivered cost. In this equation, cost becomes the target as the independent variable against which action plans are developed. It becomes a byproduct of revenue and required profits. This target costing approach is increasingly being used by B&L's automotive customers, such as Ford Motor Company, as well as other industrial companies, such as Brunswick's Mercury Marine and Caterpillar (see Chapter 16).

Complexity naturally occurs in both product and channel diversity. B&L makes some 800 standard products, plus many make-to-order items for customer specifications. Its three primary market channels are original equipment manufacturers, automotive companies, and service centers. *Nearly 80 percent of the company's sales come from 20 percent of its customers and 20 percent of B&L's product categories.*

With 800 standard products, lengthening delivery and lead times, and relatively high inventory levels, B&L identified that its customer service levels were not what the company or its customers wanted them to be. For example, stock items that are supposed to be in the warehouse when customers call, were available only 62 percent of the time. One focus of the project was to improve the existing inventory program by using new product costs and customer profitability. Customer segmenting by profitability drove changes to service levels and inventory items.

The goal of the ABC program was to support the profit planning process by focusing attention on profitable market channels, customer accounts, and products to achieve the proper mix. To do this, the company first needed to determine the relevant costs of its business processes and to identify areas of operational complexity that might have been causing inefficiencies based on the diversity of the company's product and customer base. The resulting process cost information was used to develop actual costs for key stock and make-to-order products.

As part of the ABC project, the ABC team developed a PC model that put a high priority on increasing service levels for stock accounts and, at the same time, creating more capacity for nonstock products.

Process Thinking

One of the first things the ABC team did was to identify eight cross-functional business processes—related activities performed across the company by more than one function. Using easily understood groupings, these processes include:

- determining customer needs;
- preparing and delivering quotes;
- interpreting orders for execution (schedule the mill);
- acquiring necessary resources;
- making the product;
- delivering the product;
- servicing the product; and
- obtaining administrative support (interplant and corporate sustaining).

Such identification is an important part of ABC, as it attempts to break down the traditional functional silos that control most companies. This is a key step toward implementing process thinking, a viewpoint needed in order to avoid the traditional focus on functional silos (departments), which require numerous hand-offs between departments in order to complete a particular order. The ABC team leaders described a business process focus as stapling yourself to a customer order and flowing through your organization, effectively crossing over the *white spaces* that naturally exist between departments (see Exhibit 10–2). These white spaces are often a key source of problems such as waste, inefficiency, and communication breakdowns.

Exhibit 10-2

Closing the "White Spaces"

White Spaces are the areas between functions that cause inefficiencies as processes flow through the company.

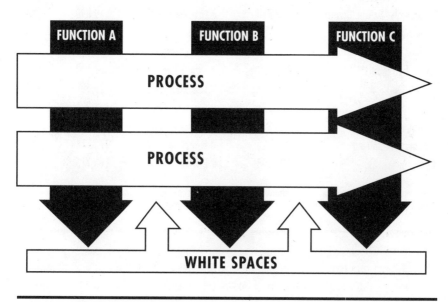

Results of Process Analysis

Total costs were determined by business process associated with a process driver. Using the 1994 volume, a unit cost can be calculated (see Exhibit 10–3 for results).

The findings were striking within every new business process. Many of the managers believed they intuitively knew where the issues were, and the ABC analysis proved them correct. In many other cases, the findings triggered new and deeper questions such as:

- What are the key value propositions (price, availability, quality, reliability, delivery, storage, order sizing, flexibility, etc.) that are important to the buying decisions of our various market channels?
- What is our quotation hit rate by customer? How can we improve?
- How do we prioritize scheduling of customer orders through the steel drawing process (first come, difficulty, order size, profitability, etc.)?
- How do we stand in the eyes of our steel suppliers? Are we a good customer to our suppliers? Do we have too many or not enough suppliers? Should we partner with our suppliers to lower costs?

Exhibit 10-3

Process Costs/Unit Costs

Business Process	Total Process Costs	Driver	1994 Volume	Unit Costs
Determine Customer Needs	$126,803	# Customers	313	$405
Prepare and Deliver Quotes	232,730	# Line Items Quoted	9,890	24
Schedule the Mill	466,738	# Shop Orders	4,861	96
Acquire Resources	836,054	# Line Items Received	5,239	160
Make the Product*	7,797,500*	# Plant #1 Tons	68,113	114*
Deliver the Product	1,835,031	# Line Items Shipped	15,697	117
Service the Product	82,538	# Customer Claims	321	257
Interplant Sustaining	2,766,834	# Interplant Tons	26,684	104
Corporate Sustaining	2,092,226	# Corporate Tons	170,116	12
Customer Specific	2,100,898	# Plant #1 Tons	68,113	31†

* This cost was further driven down to manufacturing sub-processes (blast, draw, straighten, cut, turn, grind, furnace, etc.)
† For illustration purposes only: These costs are attributable to specific customers' profitability statements.

- How competitive are our production facilities? Where are the high-impact opportunity areas within the Harvey plant and across the various plants?
- How much internal steel storage (racking) should we build and maintain to support our intended customer base?
- How do we determine the balance required between increasing manufacturing flexibility and carrying inventories?
- How many layers of supervision and control exist between the chairman's desk and the factory floor?

In the largest business process, "making the product," the ABC team found that one-third of the total plant labor time was spent waiting for materials and one-third was spent working on batch-related activities such as machine changeovers. Reducing effort spent on these two activities would provide significant opportunities to simultaneously increase capacity to achieve higher service levels and lower unit- and batch-related product costs.

The solution was not simply a matter of buying new cranes due to the limited amount of space available to store work-in-process inventory. Instead, the team focused on *what* the cranes were doing: expediting small orders, shuttling steel around limited floor space, supporting setups on the drawbenches, and shuttling products across the plant to achieve their work in process destinations.

The manufacturing representatives on the team, led by Vice President, Plant Operations Jerry Brady, attacked these issues. They examined plant layout alternatives, which resulted in expanding the capital plan to align drawbenches and shears. They supplemented critical crane needs and reconfigured existing equipment to increase its production capacity. With all of the implemented changes, operations drove the unit steel production costs to their lowest levels in years. At the same time, inventories were reduced by $2.5 million.

Other business process information is being used by the Customer Services Team, led by Senior Vice President, Sales/Marketing, Tony Romanovich, and the Business Systems Implementation Team, led by Jerry Brady and Vice President, Finance and CFO George Fleck. By having these process improvement teams led by senior management and directed by managers and directors, B&L achieves process thinking day in and day out.

Planning for Profits

As a result of the ABC implementation, B&L developed a strategy that uses business process costs to focus on products and customers. This supports the overall profit planning system in a number of ways, including:

- developing target costs for unit and batch steel processing for each product line;
- developing customer profitability profiles and goals comparing customer order patterns and measuring pretax income contributions by customer;
- identifying cost reduction opportunities and establishing prioritization rankings, implementation plans, and time lines for each opportunity.

As part of the process, B&L restated its vision, mission, strategy, and goals and deployed them through a series of strategic and operational changes. The company's policy statement changes included process modifications and equipment additions. They were designed to improve service levels and to reduce production costs by more than $1 million. The three key areas involved with this program are:

- sales/marketing initiatives that established economic order quantities (EOQ) and began reevaluating customers who buy less than one truckload of steel per year. Certain direct-ship customers should be referred to B&L's service center customers, where small bundles are regularly split and shipped.
- production initiatives that set short-term minimum runs and minimum make-to-order quantities (Economic Production Quantities or EPQ).

- inventory management initiatives that eliminated stocking/overproduction of make-to-order steel, prioritized inventory stocking requirements, reevaluated stocking items, and eliminated obsolete/slow-moving steel in the flow through racks.

Manufacturing Flexibility

Another benefit of the ABC program is that it helped B&L define its need for manufacturing flexibility. With annual carrying costs of more than $2 million on an inventory level of $25 million, B&L has the working capital and operating earnings potential to explore cycle time improvements that reduce lead times *and* inventory levels.

The company is now looking at other internal improvements to implement its flexible manufacturing strategy, such as shop floor and warehousing enhancements that help the company reduce operating costs. The impact of these changes are increased availability of stock steel, increased flexibility for producing nonstock steel, and a reduction of inventory levels on stock steel.

Actions Taken on Profitability Profiles

One of the first customer profitability profiles produced from the system was for a large original equipment manufacturer. The analysis revealed that B&L was losing $700,000 on annual shipments of 5,000 tons of steel to this customer. To rectify the situation, the chairman adopted the principle of "improve or remove" any customer company that does not generate profitable business for the company.

In preparation for the meeting with this 15-year B&L customer, the project team, led by Romanovich, developed nine scenarios, which ranged from negotiating a significant price increase to developing an exit strategy. When the meeting was being arranged, the customer told B&L, "If you are looking for a price increase, save your time and the cost of the airline tickets." Despite the dire words, B&L and the customer eventually agreed to a series of changes, including modifications to material source and pricing, process manufacturing, product testing, and pricing. The net income on the account has increased by more than $1.1 million per year, and volume on the account has nearly doubled since the changes were made. Similar work is in progress with B&L's next-largest customers. "It was an absolute home run for B&L," says Parker.

Benchmarking

Although the ABC model was developed for B&L's Harvey, Illinois, plant, the company began a benchmarking process to compare plant costs for similar operations across all of its plants. This analysis allowed B&L to identify opportunities for reducing long-term operating costs by an additional 25 percent. ABC models will be installed in each of the company's five North American plants in connection with the implementation of new integrated manufacturing planning systems.

Performance Measures

B&L followed the performance measurement development guidelines defined in *Vital Signs*, by Arthur Andersen Partner Steven Hronec. The guidelines advise simultaneous implementation of quality, cost, and time performance measures. B&L managers focused on **quality** through the automotive supplier quality programs. They focused on **time** with the elimination of waste and decreasing time in processing steel. They focused on **cost** through the implementation of ABC. During the entire process, B&L was continually concerned with maintaining the overarching goals of customer satisfaction and company profitability.

But the work did not stop there. To complete the ABC implementation process, B&L is currently:

- moving beyond product line cost information to specific product costs to eliminate the effects of product/process cost averaging;
- developing and reporting key performance indicators by business process to measure the impact of business changes and provide continuing direction towards strategic targets;
- implementing the ABC model in its other North American plants;
- developing the conceptual design of a domestic cost management system that will operate with the Oracle manufacturing/financial systems being implemented;
- reporting monthly on product/customer profitability to provide actionable feedback to sales and marketing for real-time customer/product decisions; and
- using these tools to address longer-term issues related to manufacturing flexibility and office reengineering.

Next Steps

B&L is currently pursuing further analyses that are moving them from ABC to ABM. They include:

- Increasing shop floor improvement based upon operational scenario analysis;
- Deepening analysis of office activities to drive improvement;

- Intensifying the understanding of customer-specific nuances occuring in their business processes; and
- Developing integrated linkages between the ABC model and existing subsystems.

LESSONS LEARNED

- B&L's ABC program is action-oriented in a very dynamic market. Whenever the company faced a false start in implementing the program or needed to change direction or strategy, management did so quickly.
- The company's top management was involved in all critical strategic and operational decisions. These decisions dealt largely with financial and operational matters and with customer satisfaction.
- A "Ready, Fire, Aim" philosophy needs to be applied to decision making in the organization. Overanalysis and delays in implementing ABC information paralyze improvement initiatives.
- It is essential to involve customers and obtain the necessary information about customer satisfaction in order to take appropriate action.
- While cost information is important, the real issue is that unwelcome product cost news, like "my costs are too high," must stimulate changes in strategy and operations.
- With ABC, there are two paths to follow: design a product to be more profitable or accumulate product and customer information to determine which products need to be redesigned and which processes need to be reengineered.
- Be ready to see the operation involved in an entirely different light. Radically different views of products, processes, and customers will most likely result, challenging the current approach to business.

11

USING ABC TO INCREASE REVENUES

TTI, Inc.
Fort Worth, Texas

STEVE PLAYER AND MICHAEL B. KRAMER

*Steve Player is a Partner and Firmwide Director of
Cost Management with Arthur Andersen LLP in Dallas.*

Michael B. Kramer is a Manager with Arthur Andersen LLP in Dallas.

SUMMARY

Business Issues

TTI needed a way to illustrate the cost savings a customer can enjoy by using the automatic replenishment program. Such a tool would allow TTI to dramatically increase sales to large-volume buyers.

How ABM Is Being Used

Arthur Andersen developed an activity-based costing model that can be used to analyze the costs of a customer's current purchasing process and compare it to the customer's revised costs using TTI's automatic replenishment program.

Potential customers complete a template to model their own activity-based costs of purchasing TTI's products. Data input is either from the customer's actual costs or from industry norms.

TTI's Results

Sales from the automatic replenishment program grew more than 340 percent between 1993 and 1994.

The tool allows prequalification of accounts to greatly enhance the efficiency of TTI's strategic accounts sales team.

Passive components are the behind-the-scenes workhorses of the electronics industry that most consumers never see or even know about. These tiny, inexpensive nickel-and-dime parts are needed in everything from mainframe computers to CD players. But when a manufacturer's inventory runs down, and the round-the-clock assembly line's voracious appetite for parts cannot be fed, these innocuous devices can be likened to little David who felled the giant.

TTI, Inc. seems to have taken the proverbial rocks out of David's sling with a new automatic replenishment program, an advanced approach to inventory management supported by activity-based costing. It is designed to take over most traditional purchasing responsibilities and to ensure that TTI's customers never have to order new parts and never run out of parts.

Even if it sounds too good to be true, TTI's automatic replenishment program has been in place since 1990. But with recent introduction of a new activity-based costing model, TTI has begun to capture the imagination of electronics hardware manufacturers. The 24-year-old, privately-owned electronics distributor has also found that its new program is a compelling lure for attracting new customers—the newest link in TTI's long chain of innovations for providing top service in an industry that cannot tolerate delay.

TTI's Business Environment

The bulk of TTI's business is in passive components. A typical order may be for several hundred or several thousand parts with the final bill perhaps tallying less than $100. Surprisingly, TTI has excelled over the years in handling these large-volume packages of low-dollar items. Last year the sales volume for the company was in excess of $270 million.

Some of TTI's largest customers keep passive device inventories in quantities of hundreds of thousands. When production demands change or inventory of five-cent parts is depleted to the point of stalling a high-speed assembly line, even one hour of downtime can be costly. Other time delays may be caused by a replenishment purchasing process that involves many time-consuming steps and can take from eight to ten weeks to complete. The service TTI provides its customers is not based on the low price of its components. Instead it depends on having the right parts on a manufacturer's shelf when the manufacturer needs them.

Typical Manufacturer's Procurement Process

For many manufacturers, the purchasing process begins with the Manufacturing Resource Planning (MRP) system. It uses computerized planning to determine production requirements for such component parts as semiconductors, circuit boards, and passive components. Following this determination, the manufacturer may obtain competitive bids from various suppliers, complete the actual purchase orders, and work with different vendors to order the materials. When the vendor ships the new parts, the purchaser receives, inspects, and inventories each item. All of these tasks must be completed before the parts can be used. TTI's automatic replenishment program streamlines this process and reduces the purchasing cycle time to less than one week (see Exhibit 11–1).

The ABC Strategy

Before marketing its program, TTI needed more information about the program's potential cost savings and exactly how attractive it might be for customers. TTI needed to know, for example, if the system would make the same kind of sense for a customer who buys passive components twice a year as it would for one who buys them every week.

TTI asked Arthur Andersen to construct an activity-based costing tool to analyze the plan's potential costs and benefits. The project team began by first calling on some of TTI's customers. The team performed an activity analysis of

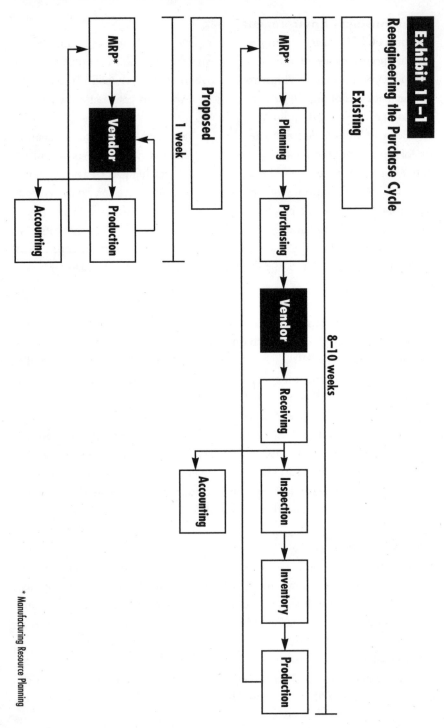

Exhibit 11-1

Reengineering the Purchase Cycle

* Manufacturing Resource Planning

all the steps and conditions involved in purchasing, stocking, and using passive components. They analyzed cost data for acquiring and using parts in a manufacturing business, including the costs of personnel, space, and computers. The percentages of materials purchased was analyzed comparing passive components to total materials on both a unit and a dollar-value basis. They interviewed individuals in accounts payable about invoicing. They examined inventories compared to production levels and calculated how fast inventories turned over. They identified the interval between a company's decision to order new parts and actual use of the parts in production.

The Simulation Template

With all of the data in hand, Arthur Andersen developed a simulation template that allows a company to compare existing cost structures dedicated to the acquisition and use of passives with the proposed automatic replenishment program. The model shows, in sequential detail, activity-based costs for how much each customer spends on scheduling, planning, purchasing, receiving, inspecting, warehousing, inventorying, and accounting.

Under the new program, TTI eliminates the majority of the non-value-added activities, reducing the 15 traditional purchasing steps to three. The MRP schedule developed by a customer to determine its production needs is downloaded electronically to TTI, which then maintains the customer's passive components inventory. TTI automatically stocks the customer's shelves in accordance with the MRP schedule for keeping the assembly lines operating. Customers do not have to place orders; the paperwork for receiving, inspecting, and matching documents is eliminated. Stocking costs and parts obsolescence are eliminated.

Although the new system doesn't focus on reducing the per-unit price a customer pays for passives, significant savings are realized from eliminating inventory, reducing administrative costs, and eliminating the costs of production delays due to lines being stopped by shortages of low-dollar parts. For example (see Exhibit 11–2), if a manufacturer is accustomed to buying these parts at a unit cost of, say, 10 cents each, he might pay 12 cents under TTI's proposed plan. But he would no longer need to keep his own inventory of passives, which in the words of one manager, "frees up a ton of cash." The investment the customer had previously dedicated to passives inventory is now available for other purposes.

In addition to the obvious liberation of cash from reduced inventory investment, TTI's automatic replenishment system yields dramatic administrative cost reductions. Due to the low-dollar nature of these parts, a company often finds

Exhibit 11-2

Manufacturer Cost Comparison

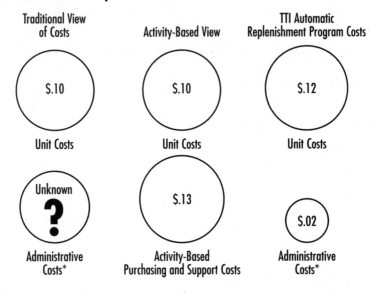

Traditional View of Costs	Activity-Based View	TTI Automatic Replenishment Program Costs
$.10	$.10	$.12
Unit Costs	Unit Costs	Unit Costs
Unknown **?**	$.13	$.02
Administrative Costs*	Activity-Based Purchasing and Support Costs	Administrative Costs*

* Administrative costs include scheduling, planning, purchasing, receiving, warehousing, inventorying, and accounting.

that the administrative costs of acquiring and stocking these parts is greater than the actual unit costs of the materials. When viewed on an ABC basis, the cost of scheduling, ordering, and receiving (13 cents) is the same for these parts as for the most expensive ones used in the factory (see Exhibit 11–3). Once this cost relationship is understood, it is clear that paying TTI a higher unit cost can be easily recovered through reduced administrative costs.

The Results

TTI piloted the ABC simulation model by offering it to five customers for testing. In the highly competitive electronics industry, in which secrecy among manufacturers is understandably the norm, TTI's customers were reluctant to share their test data. How did TTI know the new system worked and that it would be successful? All five of the test customers signed up for the automatic replenishment program.

Prior to the cost model's introduction, TTI had only seven customers using the automatic replenishment program. By aggressively using the simulation model in selling efforts, the number of customers using the automatic replenish-

Exhibit 11–3

Activity-Based Costing for Materials

Passive Components	Unit Cost = $.10
Semiconductors	Unit Cost = $5.00
Administrative Costs on Both*	$.13

Administrative Costs as % of Unit Costs

PASSIVE COMPONENTS   SEMICONDUCTORS

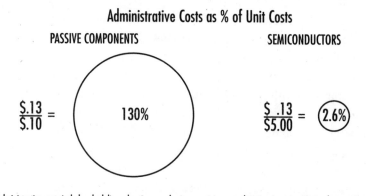

$$\frac{\$.13}{\$.10} = \boxed{130\%} \qquad \frac{\$.13}{\$5.00} = \boxed{2.6\%}$$

* Administrative costs include scheduling, planning, purchasing, receiving, warehousing, inventorying, and accounting.

ment program has grown to 31, with more than 50 expected by the end of 1995.

For TTI, the automatic replenishment program has turned out to be a significant marketing tool and a compelling argument in attracting new customers. TTI is also penetrating these accounts to a much greater level. Manufacturers who formerly dealt with a number of suppliers to acquire their passive components now deal only with TTI.

"This tool has allowed us to go to a fact-based discussion of the benefits of this approach to purchasing," states Craig Conrad, vice president, sales, for TTI. "Allowing the customers to quantify the costs and benefits using their own numbers eliminates much of the emotion from this decision. This has led to a dramatic increase in our revenues from the use of this ABC tool."

Some Pitfalls Observed

Like any good program, the automatic replenishment plan is not without some pitfalls. One concern lies in the potential for overestimating the true savings of buying passives under the new plan. For example, consider a small company that employs one purchasing agent who divides his time between buying passives and semiconductors. If you remove the agent's responsibility for buying passives under TTI's plan, then the agent will be a full-time semiconductor buyer, although buying semiconductors may only be a half-time job. Since passive components are very mature products, the shift to full-time focus on semiconductors should be a shift to higher-value activities.

If the business grows, the agent will also be available for other responsibilities. But from a pure cost reduction standpoint, the allocated costs of employees' time aren't eliminated, even though the inventory and other purchasing steps have been freed up.

In order to be economically viable for TTI, the automatic replenishment program requires a certain volume of purchases. The volume level (usually at least $500,000 in annual purchases) is necessary to cover the costs of activities assumed by TTI.

Communication within the program generally must be done electronically, which is necessary to drive processing efficiency and provide timely updates. It is a critical step in avoiding the most expensive activity in the entire process: the cost of a production line stoppage. Stoppages are greatly reduced as a customer gains the benefits of TTI's large inventory position and highly sophisticated inventory management expertise. In effect, a team of product managers focused on passives has taken over a responsibility that was once only one part of an employee's duties.

A Communications Tool

Arthur Andersen's model is actually a communications tool that helped TTI articulate what it was trying to do. TTI and its customers learned that it made intuitive sense to look at costs in detail that covers every element of purchasing passives, as presented by the ABC analysis. It provided a new way of viewing the total cost picture that had not been available before.

From the beginning, TTI's goal was to increase its customer base. The Arthur Andersen model provided cost saving evidence and was used effectively to convince customers to adopt the program. The template also quickly identified the customers that were not prime candidates, dramatically increasing the effectiveness of the strategic accounts sales force.

LESSONS LEARNED

- Customer operations personnel did not require extremely precise numbers to decide to use the program. The proper direction is more important than the precise numbers.
- Allowing the customer to input data into the template achieved much quicker acceptance. Managers are more willing to accept models they can manipulate and understand themselves.
- Linkage of the activity analysis to graphic flow charts of before-and-after data greatly enhances understanding.
- ABC techniques can be used to dramatically increase revenues in addition to reducing costs and pricing products.

12

USING ABC FOR SHARED SERVICES, CHARGE OUTS, ACTIVITY-BASED BUDGETING, AND BENCHMARKING

American Express Travel-Related Services
New York, New York

DAVID M. ALDEA AND DAVID E. BULLINGER

David M. Aldea is a Senior Manager with Arthur Andersen LLP in Toronto.
David E. Bullinger is an Experienced Manager with Arthur Andersen LLP in Dallas.

SUMMARY

Business Issues

The finance organization within the Travel-Related Services division of American Express was charged with lowering costs while encouraging improved cycle time and quality, contributing to business-unit profitability, and reducing costs by $80–$120 million.

How ABC Was Used

ABC was used to develop a charge-out model through which services and products provided by Financial Resource Centers (FRCs) could be charged directly back to the regional internal customers using them. Each FRC was to become zero-based. The model was developed so that several FRC departments could contribute to the production of a single product and customers could use any number of FRC products. ABC was then recognized and used as a valuable cost management tool. Activity-based budgeting, pay, and benchmarking systems also are being developed.

American Express' Results

American Express and Arthur Andersen have successfully linked activity-based costing with target costing, performance measurements and activity-based budgeting at its new Financial Resource Centers to create a powerful new management tool. In fact, the relatively new system has already been used to identify and implement cost reduction and process improvement initiatives.

In the early 1990s, the finance organization within the Travel-Related Services division of American Express (principally responsible for American Express card and travel transaction processing) embarked upon a new worldwide initiative, called the Challenge for Change. The group's mandate was very specific:

- Provide world-class financial services at a lower cost while encouraging improved cycle time and quality.
- Contribute to business-unit profitability where possible.
- Achieve an overall expense reduction of $80–$120 million.

Challenge for Change leaders reasoned that certain card and travel transactions that were then being processed in numerous operating centers around the world might achieve better economies of scale and service quality if they were centralized. Consequently, one of the key initiatives undertaken in support of the Challenge for Change mandates was the creation of three centralized Financial Resource Centers (FRCs). The FRCs are strategically located to support regional points of origin of transactions. An FRC in the United States services North and South America and Mexico; the United Kingdom FRC services Europe; one in India services Asia, the Middle East, Africa, Australia, and New Zealand.

Each center might be described as a transaction processing factory. Regional internal customers (a particular travel service office, for example) transfer their transaction processing requirements (such as vendors payable, payroll, bank reconciliations, etc.) to the regional FRC.

As the FRCs were put into operation, they were defined as a shared service to be used by all internal customers within each region. Internal FRC customers would vary in size and complexity, and would include all travel service offices, business travel centers, marketing departments, and other divisions operating within American Express. In return, each of the internal customers within an FRC's region would pay for its use of the FRC's transaction processing services based on its usage.

Given that each of these centers was required to charge out to the internal customer based on its consumption of FRC products or services, a service fee charge-out model was required. American Express engaged Arthur Andersen to assist in the development of an activity-based charge-out system that would meet each of the following criteria:

- Each FRC customer needed to be able to understand the charges that it incurred and how changes in its behavior would affect the costs it incurred.
- The model must include a measurement component in order to help monitor the efficiency and effectiveness with which each FRC delivered its products and services to its internal customers.
- Each FRC was to become zero-based; that is, all costs incurred by an FRC were to be charged to regional customers based on its use of the FRC's products or services.

The ABC Model Up Close

A combined American Express/Arthur Andersen team formulated a strategy that effectively adopted a model for each FRC. In essence, dollars are spent at an FRC while the FRC performs various activities that produce a series of products consumed by the FRC's various regional customers.

The model was structured so that several different departments within each FRC could contribute to the production of a single FRC product. Furthermore, each FRC customer could use a variety of different FRC products. The result was a clear, reasonable, defensible activity-based charge-out model through which FRC costs were driven directly to the customers they support (see Exhibit 12–1).

After the charge-out mandate of the project was fulfilled, the team recognized the power of the information captured by the model to help manage the costs and activities of each FRC department. Accordingly, an additional level of

Exhibit 12-1
Sample Charge-Back Invoice

Internal Charge-Back Invoice | Marketing Department
January 1995

Products Consumed	Volume	Unit Cost	Total Charge
Payroll Checks	65	$3.25	$211.25
Payroll Inquiries	22	18.25	401.50
Time Sheet Error Correction	40	55.00	2,200.00
Total Charge-Back			$2,812.75

activity analysis was performed within each department (see Exhibit 12–2).

The new cost management approach was quickly recognized as an improvement over traditional cost management techniques. As a result, department leaders were given a tool to help them create a link between department costs incurred and the changing level of activities within the department.

Further enhancements were made to separate activities defined as cost-of-poor-quality from value-added activities and to distinguish their related contribution to product costs from costs that are core to the production of the products themselves. The result was a calculation of the unit cost reduction potential that might result from improving the FRC processes, specifically by reducing non-value-added activities, including the number of rework situations.

Exhibit 12-2
Cost Management Approaches Compared

Traditional Departmental View		Activity-Based Costing View	
Postage	$378,000	Gather Payroll Time Sheets	$375,000
Bank Fees	178,000	Calculate Payroll for Period	222,000
Salaries and Benefits	149,000	Process Electronic Funds Transfers	117,000
Occupancy	51,000	Distribute Payroll	30,000
Data Processing	17,000	Process Tax Filings	22,000
Materials and Supplies	12,000	Respond to Employee Inquiries	18,000
Printing/Stationery	8,000	Correct Key Punch Errors	9,000
TOTAL	$793,000		$793,000

The Implementation Strategy

Implementation itself took approximately eight months. The American Express/Arthur Andersen team attributed much of its success to certain key guidelines that were followed throughout the implementation. They included:

- use of a joint full-time team throughout the implementation;
- inclusion of consultants and American Express personnel who were equipped with the appropriate skills on the team;
- transfer of activity-based costing expertise from Arthur Andersen personnel to American Express personnel;
- provision of nomenclature, business issues, and general guidance by American Express personnel, which significantly reduced the amount of time spent searching for information;
- assignment of a full-time information systems person to help determine how to integrate the model into existing systems and how to capture the financial and statistical data required to populate the model;
- development of a comprehensive training program for FRC personnel as well as internal customers to ensure a smooth transition from the old cost management framework to the new activity-based charge-out framework (a train-the-trainer case-study approach was chosen, which used practical business situations to demonstrate the power of the new information);
- involvement of FRC management in the design and implementation of the model (managers made numerous presentations to FRC personnel and internal customers, giving them the chance to take personal ownership in the improved approach to FRC management and charge outs); and
- recognizing enthusiastic suggestions without delaying the initial implementation plan by recording requested enhancements in a log and factoring them into a second-phase implementation plan.

Results at American Express

The first phase of the ABC engagement, activity-based charge-outs, was so successful that the joint American Express/Arthur Andersen team elected to undertake an examination of the FRCs' budget process using activity-based budgeting. The team aimed to determine whether improvements to the budget process could be made using activity-based management, reasoning that if cost center expense line items could be driven through the ABC model to products consumed by customers, a link backward through the model was also possible. In this view, customers of each FRC forecast their consumption of FRC products and services for the coming period; FRC department managers then translate that volume of consumption back into cost center budgets for each FRC department (see Exhibit 12–3 for the process flow in deriving an activity-based budget amount).

Exhibit 12–3

Activity-Based Budget Derivation

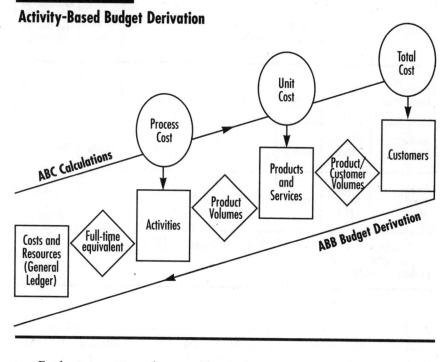

Furthermore, given a forecasted level of internal customer consumption, an activity-by-activity analysis of each department allowed process improvement savings to be factored into the forecasted costs of each department.

Activity-Based Performance Measurement and Benchmarking

Since the ABC model results in a unit cost for each product produced within the FRCs, it follows that each unit cost can be compared among different periods, internally to other similar departments within the corporation, or externally to other companies. Therefore, assuming that an FRC achieved a unit cost target (possibly set in comparison to some available world-class benchmark), rewards or special compensation arrangements can also be set up (see Exhibit 12–4 for an example of an activity-based perfromance measurement model).

Exhibit 12-4

Activity-Based Performance Measurement Model

Where do you
want to be?
▼

Activities	KPI Formula	Period Measured	Business Risk Monitored	"Normal" Value	Acceptable Range	Target Value	Recommended Action If KPIs Fall Outside Acceptable Range
Produce Payroll Check	Unit Cost/ period	Monthly	COST	$1.55	<$1.70	$1.00	Immediately examine COQ* activities and correct
Rework Due to Keying Errors	# Errors/ Volume	Monthly	QUALITY	1 in 6,000	>1 in 5,500	1 in 10,000	Determine cause, refocus training
Produce Payroll Check	Units Processed/ FTE†	Monthly	PRODUCTION	25,000	>23,000	>26,000	Root cause analysis, review FTE† per activity

Key Performance Indicators (KPI)

* Cost of Quality
† Full-time equivalent

For example, analysis might reveal that it costs one FRC $4.50 to produce a payroll check, but the method used by another FRC, identified as a best practice, only costs $2.57. Identification of the less expensive method as a best practice and implementation of it across all FRCs would bring the unit cost down. In this way, ABC can lead to benchmarking and best-practices analyses that feed back to target costing and link to performance measurements.

Conclusion

After these three additional processes are implemented, American Express' Financial Resource Centers' activity-based costing model will have completed the transition to a true activity-based management initiative.

LESSONS LEARNED

- The commitment of a talented implementation team is essential to the success of the project.
- From a technological standpoint, it is important to develop the ABC model within the company's existing infrastructure.
- Creative methods of simplifying the data collection and distribution process ensured that the model's implementation did not significantly disrupt existing business operations.
- A comprehensive training program for the model's eventual owners as well as the users of the information is key.
- Solid project management skills, even more than technical ABC skills, are imperative for quality project delivery and client commitment.
- It is important to resist the temptation to design and implement a "do everything" model; break up the project into phases, which allows for achieved successes to be built upon and functionality requests by users of the information to be incorporated.
- It is important to realize that the ABC model need not reinvent the wheel that other systems already accomplish.
- Frequent update meetings enable upper management to demonstrate continued support of successful implementation and provide a forum in which management assistance can be solicited and issues resolved as they develop.
- The client needs to remain focused on the benefits of the program and should link ABC with known corporate initiatives and objectives.

13

USING ABM TO UNDERSTAND TELECOMMUNICATIONS MAINTENANCE AND PROVISIONING PROCESSES

Telecommunications Corporation*

RICHARD STOREY AND ELLEN FITZPATRICK

*Richard Storey is a Partner with Arthur Andersen LLP in New York.
Ellen Fitzpatrick is a Senior Manager with Arthur Andersen LLP in Chicago.*

* Telecommunications Corp. is a fictitious name for a real company; the case study describes actual events.

SUMMARY

Business Issues

With increasing competition throughout the Telecommunications Corp. service territory, Telecommunications Corp. needed to better understand the costs of various business processes. Then Telecommunications Corp. managers could look at the key drivers of these costs and how they relate to various products, customers, and service areas.

The prototype activity-based costing models developed for two of Telecommunications Corp.'s service areas were designed for adoption throughout Telecommunications Corp.'s six-state service area and provide for full-scale use of activity-based management.

How ABC/ABM Were Used

The joint Telecommunications Corp./Arthur Andersen ABC team developed models for two key business processes—maintenance and provisioning—for certain geographic markets.

The purpose of the project was to:

- provide market area managers with relevant cost information for activities over which they had control;
- develop an ABM prototype for one market area that could be used to demonstrate the direct linkage between tactical decisions and cost consequences;
- develop an ABC methodology and process that could be rolled out to all Telecommunications Corp. market areas at a later date.

The Results for Telecommunications Corp.

Although the initial ABC/ABM projects ended after completion of the first prototype, Telecommunications Corp. is now positioned to develop ABC models and implement ABM throughout its entire service area when the company determines that the internal business climate is appropriate.

Telecommunications Corp. is a telecommunications service provider that provides local exchange services across a six-state area. Telecommunications Corp. determined that it needed to know the costs to serve its customers; which products drive the costs; and what the key drivers of the costs are.

The company had long relied on general ledger data for information about labor costs, occupancy, training, supplies, and the like. In addition, systems had been developed to look at customer and product profitability, but they were based on allocations of costs to products and customers. These allocations were based on high-level assumptions (such as an order is an order, whether for one product or 30) that did not accurately represent the true cost drivers.

Arthur Andersen was engaged to help Telecommunications Corp. develop a prototype activity-based costing model that could be used for cost management, identifying activity costs, and providing a basis for process improvement. Telecommunications Corp. had completed research on ABC and ABM, but had not yet determined how these tools would work within their business environment. The company wanted to use the initial prototype as an educational tool to demonstrate the benefits of ABC.

ABC Prototype

The prototype was developed for the maintenance process of one of Telecommunications Corp.'s market areas using existing data from the financial and operations systems (see Exhibit 13–1 for the conceptual framework). In addition to supplying relevant cost information, the prototype would also demonstrate to operations managers the linkage between tactical decisions and cost consequences. The plan was to expand the prototype to include Telecommunications Corp. market areas.

All of Telecommunications Corp.'s customers in the geographic area chosen for the prototype are served through one of 15 wire centers. When a residential or business customer calls with a service problem, maintenance personnel from the associated wire center complete the required work and assign a disposition code indicating the type of service problem. Similarly, when a customer calls to order new service, provisioning personnel associated with the wire center fulfill the order.

Exhibit 13–1

The ABM Conceptual Framework Used

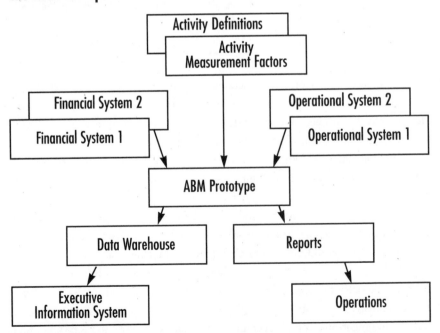

Ultimately, the ABC prototype focused on both the maintenance and provisioning processes. It was designed to determine activity costs across the wire centers, enabling Telecommunications Corp. to:

- see the end-to-end process costs at an activity level;
- understand the actual drivers of activity costs;
- compare the costs of each wire center;
- understand why various wire centers' costs might differ;
- find out how each wire center might improve; and
- calculate key performance indicators to be used for performance measurement.

Telecommunications Corp.'s managers would be able to perform "what if" scenarios, calculations that reveal how costs would be affected by process changes or changes in transaction volumes. They could also compare operational and financial information across wire centers and "turfs" (to understand differences in costs and activities) and identify high-cost activities (so that initiatives toward work simplification and reengineering could be taken).

Strategy

To implement Telecommunications Corp.'s ABC system over a period of six months, a joint Telecommunications Corp./Arthur Andersen team conducted interviews and focus groups with operational personnel to identify the maintenance and provisioning activities as well as the time spent performing them. The team itemized the information in an activity dictionary and documented it in process maps, which defined the maintenance-related activities performed by each functional organization and highlighted the hand-offs or outputs to other functional organizations in the maintenance and provisioning processes (see Exhibit 13–2 for a sample map). The maps served as the framework for building the ABC model.

In order to build the model and have it be useful on an ongoing basis, several additional steps were taken:

- determining the specific sources of data required and the methods for extracting it;
- preparing a schematic of the ABM prototype, validating the data, and building the prototype using selected software;
- developing reports generated from the ABM prototype and preparing technical documentation for maintaining the model in the future;
- training Telecommunications Corp. employees to run and update the ABM prototype; and

Exhibit 13-2

Sample Process Map

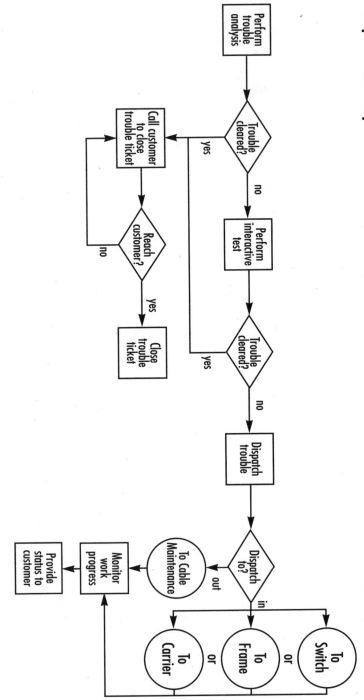

- developing a work plan and schedule for rolling out ABM to the rest of the Telecommunications Corp. organization.

Software Flexibility

Upon completion of the ABC prototype, Telecommunications Corp. asked Arthur Andersen to develop ABC models for a second strategic business unit. During the course of the second project, the team moved to a new software package that had greater capacity and flexibility and would fit better within the Telecommunications Corp. environment for continuous use.

The change was prompted by the large number of functional departments involved in the end-to-end maintenance process. The first software utilized required a separate model for each department; with the new program, all of the functional departments could be combined in one ABC model, producing a more comprehensive look at costs across all of these organizations.

After the Pilot

Although the ABC prototype provided the foundation for generating ongoing reports of cost data and information, several issues arose during the course of the pilot that effectively stalled the project in the pilot stage. The project and project team lacked the critical support from upper management; without this support, it was difficult to position the project and emphasize the relevance to all employees.

This lack of management sponsorship also contributed to the project team's inability to sell the prototype and its capabilities to operations. Operations personnel were focused on service, and largely unconcerned about cost. Significant change management needs to occur before these personnel will see the relevance of ABC information.

The project team also relied on part-time team members rather than a full-time client team. Although the team members contributed their time and expertise, as available, they also maintained their corporate job functions. A full-time client-based project coordinator or leader was not available to ensure that the projects reached their intended goals.

While the project has yet to transition to mainstream, the prototypes will enable Telecommunications Corp. managers to demonstrate the benefits of ABC and ABM and provide a system that can eventually be replicated throughout Telecommunications Corp.'s service areas. A key to moving forward is understanding just how this ABM approach will help meet Telecommunications Corp.'s business objectives in a cost beneficial manner.

LESSONS LEARNED

- The ABC implementation team must consist of employees with skills and backgrounds in finance and operations, and who can make more than a part-time commitment to the project. Some of the team members need to be experts in understanding the company's operational support systems and business processes.

- Defining the type and volume of information that will be imported from other databases, understanding where the information comes from, and making sure it is accurate, meaningful, and complete is one key to the success of an ABM project.

- Informing and educating the affected employees at all levels in the organization is important, especially when resistance to change is a critical factor.

- Senior management's visible commitment to the project from the beginning is essential.

- When ABC is being introduced to a company for the first time, any changes in direction need to be evaluated; determine which "distractions" take priority over the core project.

14

ADVANCED USE OF ABM — USING ABC FOR TARGET COSTING, ACTIVITY-BASED BUDGETING, AND BENCHMARKING

AT&T Paradyne Corporation
Largo, Florida

Jay Collins

Jay Collins is a Senior Manager with Arthur Andersen LLP in Tampa;
he was formerly an employee of AT&T Paradyne Corp.

SUMMARY

Business Issues

Shortly after AT&T Paradyne became a wholly owned subsidiary of AT&T, management, taking into account the following factors, identified the need for ABM:

- Product designs, which establish more than 85 percent of product cost, had to continually incorporate the latest in technology.
- Products were becoming smaller, more customer-specific, and far more expensive to manufacture.
- Manufacturing, employing a factory mall concept, was shifting from labor-intensive operations to high-tech automated machine-assembly operations.
- The existing accounting system was no longer of value in supporting strategic, operational, and financial life-cycle decisions.
- Time-to-market was compressing, as was the window for realizing profits.
- Formation of multiple Customer Business Units resulted in gross allocations of cost that provided no line-of-sight understanding.

How ABM Was Used

The ABM initiative focused on calculating more accurate product cost so that design engineering, product management, and manufacturing team members could use the information for decision making. Since inventory was valued using activity cost, the ABM system not only provided information for strategic and operational decisions but for financial decisions as well. Production Engineering went as far as incorporating ABM targets into its performance review process.

In addition, monthly ABC product cost information was used in an ABM target costing program to project future activity and product costs. AT&T Paradyne's initial ABC project led to activity-based management, activity-based budgeting, and activity-based benchmarking programs.

AT&T Paradyne's Results

Says the ABM/ABC team leader, "We are using ABM as a means to execute our strategic management process, in order to ascertain the total value we provide our customers. Total value is determined through ABM by using a balanced approach in combining ABC, quality, and delivery performance of our products and services."

As the ABM process matured at AT&T Paradyne, the company began to experience a cultural change. ABM made it clear that understanding and managing activities is key to advancing manufacturing strategy (see Exhibit 14–1).

Exhibit 14-1

Strategic Management Process

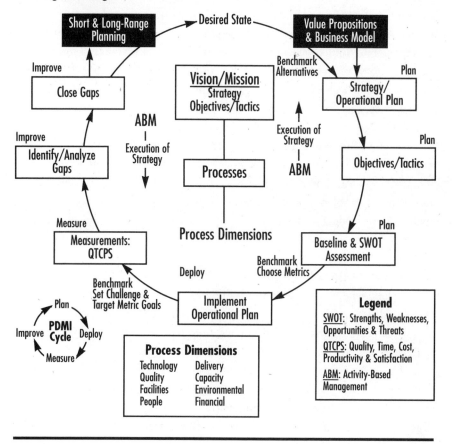

In February, 1989, AT&T acquired Paradyne Corporation, a company specializing in data communications equipment and services. The company designs and produces medium- and high-speed data communications equipment, which provides an interface between telephone networks and computers. Headquartered on the west coast of Florida, the company employs approximately 2,000 people and generates about $400 million in annual sales. Its mission is to "lead in multimedia network access products and technology," securing a strong, defensible, and profitable position in the $4-billion network access market.

The Business Environment

AT&T Paradyne's old cost system assigned support and production overhead costs to products as a percentage of materials and direct labor. Clearly, with all the changes taking place in the industry, AT&T Paradyne's old system could no longer provide an accurate means of determining the true cost of products. For example overcosting of older products resulted in the appearance of lower-than-expected margins. These products, because they required more direct labor assembly hours, were assigned a large amount of overhead or support cost, even though they were in the mature or declining stage of their life cycle and therefore did not require as much overhead resource.

On the other hand, newer products designed to need fewer direct labor hours received a much smaller amount of support cost even though they required a great deal of attention. Allocating cost based on material cost caused just as many problems, only in reverse. The more a product's material cost—such as new products—the more overhead it received, even though in many instances the true cost had nothing to do with volume or the cost of material.

Moving to ABM: Using ABC

AT&T Paradyne was an early and leading-edge ABM pioneer. In 1990, when ABM and ABC were just starting to become recognized by the industry, AT&T Paradyne, realizing the value of moving from its traditional cost system to an activity-based system, jumped on the ABC bandwagon.

One of the biggest benefits of moving to ABC was the ability to provide the company's design and production engineers with the cost information they needed in the ever-so-important early stages of product development. Determining end-product costs, as well as other features such as product safety, process cycle time, and quality, early on was important.

Strategy

As a first step, AT&T Paradyne developed a basic ABC model using two drivers: volume measured by number of units and by part number for non-volume-related expenses. For example, calculating a cost-per-part number of about $1,000 led to very high reported costs for low-volume products that had many unique components. The system proved to be too simplistic, overcosting products that had multiple variations. Since the company had eliminated its direct labor-based standard cost system, large differences in product costs became highly visible. Adopting the two-driver ABC system also caused dramatic swings in inventory dollars, since the new system was also being used to evaluate inventory.

Soon after the basic model was developed, a cross-functional ABM team was formed to make improvements to it and move forward with ABM. The team consisted of members with engineering, marketing, systems, and finance backgrounds. The team developed a model that interfaces with the general ledger and various manufacturing and planning systems (see Exhibit 14–2).

Exhibit 14–2

ABC Collection and Calculation

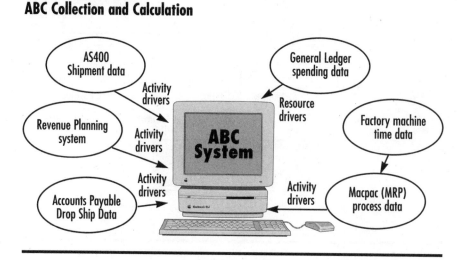

Improvements to the ABC model included: assigning production costs using activity drivers such as number of insertions, number of parts, and test hours; assigning support costs based on drivers such as the number of change orders, uniqueness by product family, and type of quality audit; and segregating raw-material support costs into various purchased-part groupings for assigning materials acquisition costs.

The new ABC model (see Exhibit 14–3) consisted of four major cost elements (material, material acquisition, production, and support), forty-four cost pools, and thirteen activity drivers. (See Exhibit 14–4 for the cost breakdown and resulting Bill of Activities.)

The critical nature of the ABC initiative helped design engineers get the information they needed in order to supplement quality and time constraints with manufacturing and purchasing considerations so they could make accurate ABM decisions. The ABM team improved the model during each of the next two years. Today, the ABC process has stabilized and is well-established and accepted within the company's engineering and manufacturing operations. With

Exhibit 14–3

ABC Model of Cost Flows in Building a Modem

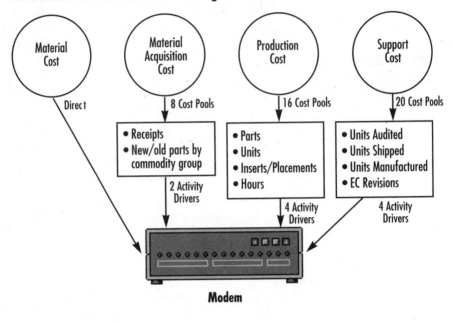

Exhibit 14–4

Example of a Modem's Cost Breakdown and Bill of Activities

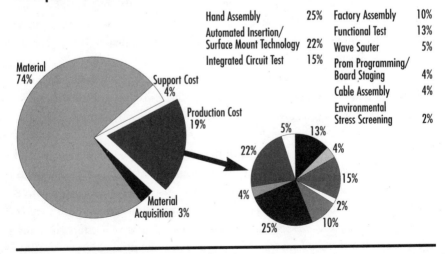

the new system reporting actual ABC product costs monthly, the team has advanced to the next step, activity-based target costing.

Using Target Costing and Benchmarking

An ABC target costing process was established for all new and major existing products to facilitate life-cycle cost management. The target costing process begins with marketing managers estimating the price at which a new product with specified features and functionality can be sold to achieve a significant market position. From there, product and manufacturing associate teams inter-lock on a targeted product cost that is a buildup of material and activity cost.

With this ABC information, AT&T Paradyne benchmarks activity costs, which compares the company's leading-edge concepts to find out how competi-tive its products are with other best-in-class companies. A company team mem-ber says, "When you target certain activity costs based on benchmarking, you know how competitive you are and where you need to improve."

ABM Detailed Results

Product managers can now discuss design decisions with engineers, and encour-age them to use standard and fewer components, reducing the number of vendors.

Another major procedural change that resulted from ABM was reallocation of facility costs. Prior to ABC implementation, facility costs for the company were allocated to functional areas based on square feet; as a result, manufactur-ing was receiving more cost than it was consuming. The higher cost was reflect-ed in cost of goods sold or product cost, artificially lowering product margins as well as increasing inventory costs. With ABC, facility cost was pooled into office space, manufacturing and warehouse space, and unused space. Highlighting facility-allocated cost identified overcosting of the company's cost of goods sold by more than $500,000. The information was useful in decision making as it enabled management to identify and address the issue of unused space.

AT&T Paradyne did not use its ABC system solely for special studies, as many companies do. Team members produced monthly reports on the actual incurred costs of products and processes, allowing management to use the num-bers to value inventory for external reporting.

The company has now extended ABC to create an activity-based budgeting process. AT&T Paradyne is able to look at product volume forecasts and back-logs, which in turn determine the activity level. With this information, an activ-ity cost is set, giving manufacturing the ability to predict a desired spending level. This information can also be compared to that of the previous two years, showing what spending decisions have been influenced and how those decisions correlate back to the products and gross margins they have affected.

AT&T Paradyne Moving Forward

Team members, from design engineers to product manufacturing managers, now have ownership in understanding costs. This has resulted in better decisions in all areas. The company's marketing group is now piloting an ABC project to identify the most cost-effective distribution strategy. Customer administration is also looking to use ABC in its service-level agreement process. Manufacturing will continue improving both the ABC model as well as the reports generated, since cost performance continues to be a key measurement in the manufacturing strategy.

LESSONS LEARNED

- Any major undertaking, such as moving to ABM, requires commitment and dedication from a high-level sponsor as well as a relentless champion.
- To be successful, teams need to involve various skilled individuals. This is not just an accounting exercise; financial decisions are only part of the equation.
- ABM supports strategic decisions, such as pricing, mix, make versus buy, and the kinds of investments that are needed.
- ABC improves the concurrent engineering process by increasing cost awareness in design decisions.
- ABC enhances ability to benchmark activities, drivers, and cost data against best-in-class competitors.
- Linking the ABC manufacturing efforts with budgeting, inventory valuation, and performance evaluation will accelerate integration of ABC into the management of the company.

15

INCREASING CUSTOMER AND STAKEHOLDER SATISFACTION, AND SUPPORTING BENCHMARKING AND PERFORMANCE MEASUREMENT WITH ABM

AT&T Business Communications Services
Manassas, Virginia

TERRENCE B. HOBDY

*Terrence B. Hobdy is a Manager with Arthur Andersen LLP in Dallas;
he was formerly an employee of AT&T Business Communications Services.*

SUMMARY

Business Issues

With the breakup of the regional Bell operating companies and increasing deregulation, all telecommunications companies face an increasingly complex and competitive environment. Achieving low-cost, highly efficient processes is a key to success. Industry leader AT&T has recognized that it is critically important to implement financial processes that will provide more meaningful cost information to support operational decisions. Activity-based management is one such tool which has been successfully applied within AT&T.

In particular, ABM provides valuable operational cost information regarding the performance of AT&T Business Communications Services' (BCS) Virtual Telecommunications Network Service (VTNS). VTNS provides integrated services and value-added functionality to more than 250 of AT&T BCS's largest customers.

How ABM Was Used

Specifically, ABM has been implemented in a number of AT&T BCS customer care centers. Employees in these centers perform customer care activities such as provisioning, maintenance, and billing. This case reports how ABM was implemented in the Manassas, Virginia, Business Billing Center (BBC). The BBC consists of the Billing Control Office, which performs activities such as processing service orders and performing billing adjustments, and the Bill Print Center, which prints, sorts, and distributes bills to customers.

The Results at AT&T BCS

The implementation of ABM within the business billing center has provided management with relevant and reliable cost information. The cost information has also been used to support activity-based budgeting and provided a foundation for supporting benchmarking efforts. By having access to reliable cost data, management can investigate cost discrepancies and more effectively plan process improvement efforts to achieve required cost reductions.

Since the divestiture of the regional Bell operating companies (RBOCs) from AT&T in 1984, the business environment for the United States telecommunications industry has changed significantly. The profound changes that followed deregulation, coupled with changes in economics, technology, and customer demand, have created a new, more competitive landscape for the lucrative $70-billion long distance market. Today, more than 500 companies compete in the long-distance service market. Although AT&T maintains a 60 percent market share of the United States long distance market, its dominant position will be seriously threatened once RBOCs are allowed to compete for long distance customers. Long distance carriers will also be allowed to compete for local customers. Additionally, cable companies and European firms have created strategic alliances with established domestic telecommunications companies with the approval of the FCC. Telecommunications may well be the world's most competitive industry.

Today's competitive business environment dictates that companies competing in this industry provide services as cost efficiently as possible. Traditionally, FCC regulators calculated tariffs for services based on companies' cost plus allowed profit. The profit objectives were primarily based on a company's cost structure and a predetermined return on investment. Thus, many companies within the telecommunications industry, such as AT&T, developed cost allocation schemes to assign costs to services. These allocation schemes were principally designed to meet regulatory requirements as opposed to business needs.

Scope of the ABM Project

Prior to implementing ABM, the BBC used a high-level allocation method to assign costs (see Exhibit 15–1). For example, various BBC functional work groups reported the amount of hours expended performing activities on a weekly basis to the BBC financial reporting group. The financial reporting group calculated activity costs by dividing the total expenses for the work group by the percentage of time spent performing that activity. In essence, the center used an aggregate total cost pool allocated on a single driver percent of time. Next, unit costs for the activity were calculated by dividing total costs for the activity by activity volumes.

Exhibit 15–1

Allocation Method of Cost Assignment

Work Group A
Total Monthly Expenditures: $ 100,000

Activity	% Time	Activity Cost	Volume	Unit Cost
Process Orders	40	$ 40,000	2,000	$20
Sort Bills	60	60,000	5,000	$12
	100%	$100,000		

Note: These numbers are for illustrative purposes only and are not representative of the company.

Although the allocation methodology was sufficient for calculating high-level activity and unit costs, the resulting data was not reliable for operational decision-making purposes. The older method was simplistic in that it assumed that all costs moved based on the percent of time expended. There was little data about the cost of services. As a result of these aggregate allocations, the cost data was less than adequate.

The activity-based management project included several areas. Business billing center management and nonmanagement employees were included in the project's scope. Costs for all headquarters staff who supported the BBC were included as well.

Executive management formed a cross-functional team consisting of staff from the Manassas, Virginia, BBC headquarters, line organizations, and Business Communications Services finance department staff to accomplish the following operational business needs:

- Provide operational performance results regarding the time, quality, and cost of activities and processes (e.g., service order process) performed within the BBC.
- Provide reliable results that could be utilized for business planning, budgeting, and supplier-customer (internal) funding negotiations.
- Benchmark the BBC's costs with other billing centers and internal BBC work groups.

Operating Within the Values of the Company

Successful implementation of ABM within the BBC required the project implementation team to operate within AT&T's five common bond values: teamwork, innovation, integrity, dedication to the customer, and respect for the individual. Teamwork was a key ingredient to the successful completion of the project. The cross-functional ABM project team formed by executive management exhibited teamwork by partnering with other stakeholders. For example, core team members met with representatives from the service order process management team to discuss and identify their cost information requirements. The service order team specifically requested cost information regarding rework activities for service order rejects. The unit cost data would be especially valuable for allowing the process management team to prepare cost/benefit analyses for implementing system enhancements to reduce the number of rejected service orders.

Innovation and integrity also were demonstrated during the implementation of ABM in the BBC. For example, new data interface tools were developed to mechanize the importing of operational data such as activity volumes into the cost model. The project team maintained the highest level of integrity by developing good documentation and audit trails to support the preparation of financial and operational data. This effort assured that the unit cost results would be both reliable and accurate.

Dedication to helping the customer was also demonstrated through the training. The training allowed the project team members to acquire a conceptual understanding of ABM, learn the implementation methodology, and obtain hands-on experience using the ABM costing software. This training helped educate the internal users of the system. In effect management is the internal customer of the information provided by this system. Training also helped them to understand how ABM could be used and how it would support managing external customers.

The final common bond value manifested during the project was respect for the individuals. Specifically, input from all levels of the organization from upper management to nonmanagement personnel was given equal credibility. Each individual's input was highly valued regardless of position or level. Additionally, the project team consisted of a diverse group of people, reflecting the diversity of the BBC.

Implementing the New ABM Cost System

The ABM project team followed an established methodology for implementing ABM. The approach used Sapling's NetProphet® software tool and followed their eight-step methodology for implementing ABM. It was successfully employed during the nine-week project (see Exhibit 15–2).

Exhibit 15–2

Sapling's Eight-Step Methodology

Step	Task
1	Define the project scope.
2	Identify activities, resources, and drivers.
3	Build the cost schematic.
4	Collect data.
5	Build the cost model.
6	Validate the cost model.
7	Interpret new cost information.
8	Perform "what if" analysis.

Activities were specifically defined at an operational level to provide cost information for process improvement efforts. The model statistics were further detailed by the Billing Control Office and Bill Print Center (see Exhibit 15–3).

Exhibit 15–3

Summary of Model Statistics

	Billing Control Office	Bill Print Center
Activities	139	116
Accounts	39	36
Major Processes	4	4
Cost Objects	7	7

Cost Information and Process Improvement

The implementation of ABM within the BBC has provided management with relevant and reliable cost information. From a cost perspective, activity and unit cost information is available for all services supported by the BBC including the unit cost for processing a service order (see Exhibit 15–4 for an example).

Exhibit 15–4

Process Service Order Activity Unit Cost

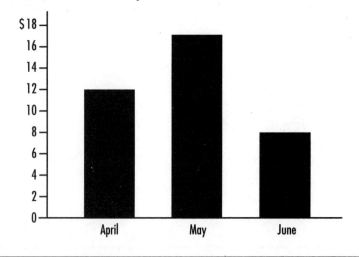

Such unit cost information is very beneficial for process improvement efforts. A definition of the process management structure will further clarify this concept. The VTNS process management model consists of eight major processes:

- product development;
- product delivery;
- product marketing;
- sales;
- network operations;
- billing operations;
- field sales; and
- contract management.

Process owners were selected and empowered with accountability for the operational performance, customer satisfaction, and financial performance for the eight major processes. The activity process service order in Exhibit 15–4 is one of many activities for process 5.0, the network operations process. Using this system, activity and unit costs performed in the BBC in support of the network operations process can be provided to BBC management, product management, and the network operations process owner on a monthly basis. Cost reduction ideas can be evaluated to determine the impact on the cost and frequency of activities within the Network Operations process. When implemented, these improvements can be tracked to ensure that they are realized.

Additionally, the cost information has been used to support activity-based budgeting. For example, product management forecasts 100 new large customers for the next year and historical volume data correlates 20 service orders per new customer. Therefore, BBC management can calculate the costs associated for processing an additional 2,000 service orders (100 customers x 20 orders/customer).

Also, the unit cost can be broken into separate expense categories such as wages/salaries, benefits, telecommunications, building rents, and building services. Activities can be noted by management and nonmanagement level employees. Using the new ABM cost model, the BBC can plan necessary resource and staffing requirements intelligently. Incremental additional resources can be determined. Thus, budgeting, planning, and funding negotiations are supported with fact-based cost information regarding activity driver volumes and costs.

Similar analyses can be performed for other activities including those of the bill print center. As a result, a more comprehensive view of budgeted costs is provided to all stakeholders.

The unit cost information also provides a foundation for supporting benchmarking efforts. Unit costs are used as metrics for benchmarking internal work groups as well as comparing the BBC to other billing centers. Work groups that are more cost efficient at performing an activity can share information with other internal groups and billing centers. By having access to reliable cost data, management can investigate cost discrepancies and more effectively plan process improvement efforts to achieve cost reductions.

Additionally, benchmarks were developed to measure the time required for performing activities such as processing a service order (see Exhibit 15–5 for an example comparing three work groups).

Exhibit 15–5

Process Service Order Activity—Processing Times

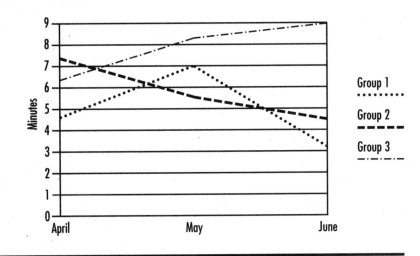

Activity process times were used to benchmark with internal BBC work groups and other billing centers as well. More importantly, the benchmarking data supported key process improvements such as the development of on-line access to the ordering system. This system enhancement allowed BBC associates to review the service order reports on-line, thereby significantly reducing paper costs within the center. Cost savings from this process improvement were in excess of $40,000 per month.

These two examples illustrate how management used activity and unit cost data to perform benchmarking analyses, reduce cycle times, and achieve cost reductions. ABM also enabled the BBC to implement significant cost reductions despite increases in customer volume growth. While the volume of minutes of use grew 26 percent for 1993 and 20 percent for 1994, BBC operational costs did not increase. As a matter of fact, operational costs decreased 8 percent and 18 percent, respectively, over the same period.

Results at AT&T BCS

Several benefits were derived from the successful implementation of ABM within the Manassas BBC. First, process analysis and process management, integrating with ABM, helped AT&T BCS to dramatically increase customer satisfaction for the VTNS service offering. Specifically, customer satisfaction metrics such as timeliness of bill receipt, completeness of billing information, and accuracy of the bill increased significantly.

Second, the new ABM model provided powerful cost information that was useful for managing billing center performance and costs, especially unit cost by activity and process. Benchmarking from both time and cost perspectives, along with activity-based budgeting efforts, were also supported by the ABM cost model.

Third, the implementation of ABM in this particular BBC provided a foundation for implementing ABM in numerous provisioning, billing, account inquiry, and maintenance customer care centers across the United States. The BBC ABM project team received the prestigious CFO Quality Team Award for its efforts. Additional consulting support by Arthur Andersen facilitated the roll out of ABM to other customer care centers.

Fourth, ABM helped foster a win-win relationship between finance, operations, and product management. These stakeholders received fact-based cost information that was very important for funding negotiations.

Finally, ABM established the foundation for implementing a new performance measurement framework for operational centers. Specifically, accurate and reliable activity-based costs were developed as opposed to meaningless cost allocations.

LESSONS LEARNED

- Financial management tools such as ABM can only be successful if they are implemented in lockstep with the mission, vision, values (common bond), and strategic imperatives of the company.

- Executive management along with process owner support and buy-in was critical to the successful implementation of ABM within the customer care centers.
- Stakeholders clearly articulated ABM objectives to ensure the success of the cross-functional team.
- Establishment of operations as the project leader fostered greater partnership between finance and operations.
- The investment in training for team members and the recognition of the need for continual resource requirements to support the ABM effort was also important.

Section III

Future Weapons: The Next Wave of Lessons

TARGET COSTING'S
LINK WITH ABC AND ABM

Activity-based costing and activity-based management are important tools that can support the target costing process. ABC is the cost assignment view focusing on the strategic view of cost. ABC answers the question, "What do things cost?" ABC provides information such as product, customer, and channel costing. ABM is the process view focusing on the operational view of costs. ABM answers the question, "What causes cost to occur?" ABM provides information such as process costs at particular utilization levels. Both tools can be applied on a prospective basis to estimate product and process costs in a target costing environment.

Target costing, when applied to new product development, is recursive in so far as it parallels the natural progression of product definition. During the early stages of product development, ABC can be applied effectively to estimate product cost at a general level, which is useful for preliminary evaluation of product feasibility. As product and process definition become more defined through the design process, predictive ABM process cost models can be applied to estimate the costs of particular functions and components using particular processes. The process view of cost can be particularly valuable to engineers as they work to reduce product and process cost, improve utilization of current machines and equipment, and eliminate waste and process variation. Ever more robust software tools that integrate design issues and cost information are becoming available.

Since target costing can be applied to the entire value chain, another important opportunity is to use the process view of cost with suppliers during supplier selection. This use can continue focusing on reducing the cost of purchased materials and components throughout the product life cycle. Cost planning and process planning for how logistics, customer service, and marketing processes will be implemented can be evaluated in terms of their impact on total product cost, customer satisfaction, and program profitability as well.

The following case study illustrates the link between target costing, ABC, and ABM.

16

TARGET COSTING AT CATERPILLAR

Caterpillar Inc.
Peoria, Illinois

JOHN J. DUTTON WITH REID DALTON AND JOE MCNEELY

*John J. Dutton is a Senior Manager with Arthur Andersen LLP in Dallas.
Reid Dalton and Joe McNeely are Senior Managers with
Arthur Andersen LLP in Chicago.*

SUMMARY

Business Issues

In response to intense competitive challenges from Japanese companies, Caterpillar Inc. increased target cost management for key activities and in product development programs, internally and within its supplier network. Competitive issues included product reliability, after-sales services, and increased value. Value is determined by elements such as the customer's cost to own and operate the product, the mix of features and functions in the product, and the relative quality of these elements.

What Tools Are Used

- Investing in cost awareness and assigning expenditure responsibilities to those doing the work achieved cost ownership.
- The marketing organization, through a global sales and services support group, uses techniques such as quality function deployment to determine customer needs.
- New product introduction is a principal part of Caterpillar's long-term strategy.
- The three critical process variables—quality, cost, and timing—are managed simultaneously.

Caterpillar's Results

Target costing programs have been critical to Caterpillar's ability to maintain its market leadership position; annual sales in 1994 rose to $14.3 billion, 30 percent above 1989 sales.

For most of its 70-year history, Caterpillar Inc., headquartered in Peoria, Illinois, has enjoyed its well-deserved reputation as a premier manufacturer of heavy-duty earth movers. The distinctive, bright yellow Cat machines are visible at major construction sites around the world.

However, about a decade ago, a Japanese manufacturer began making deep inroads in the heavy equipment marketplace with highly reliable and cost-competitive products. Even though market-share gains were generally being made at the expense of other Caterpillar competitors, price pressure was seriously eroding Caterpillar's profitability. The powerful technique used by the Japanese competitor to support its major market penetration was target costing.

Target costing is an advanced cost management tool for developing and delivering the products customers want while reducing total product costs through the life cycle (see Exhibits 16–1 and 16–2) The exhibits suggest key target costing principles. Early investment in product development is less costly during the product life cycle and it has a greater effect on product cost, quality, and development cycle time.

The target costing process is a multifunctional management method that

Exhibit 16–1

Effort Expended in Each Life Cycle Stage

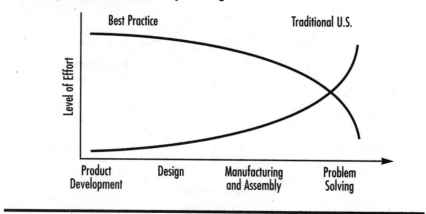

Exhibit 16–2

Opportunity for Improvement and Cost of Changes by Life Cycle Stage

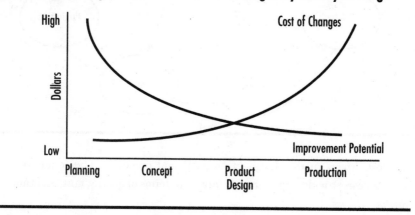

depends on the combined help of the production, engineering, research and development, marketing, and finance departments.

Responsibility and accountability are at the heart of Caterpillar's multi-functional New Product Introduction (NPI) teams (see Exhibit 16–3). These teams are responsible for delivering reliable, quality products on time, within target costs, and achieving sales as well as market-share goals. Frequently, cost comparisons across product lines are conducted to identify solutions and evalu-

Exhibit 16-3

The Multi-functional New Product Introduction Team

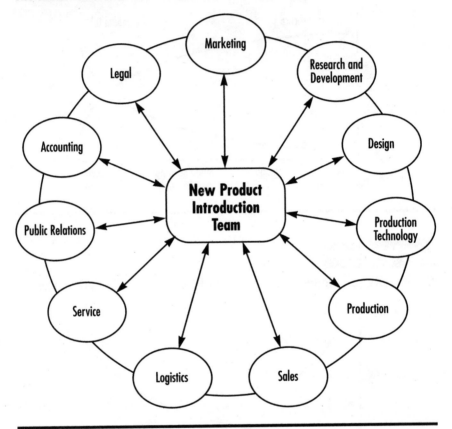

ate cost drivers in the design of products and processes. The results of such analyses can provide important advantages in terms of quality, cost, and time-to-market.

Caterpillar's target costing process is, in essence, a management-by-policy program. Instead of delegating responsibility and "just steering the ship," as one executive puts it, the firm provides true leadership in terms of deciding what is important in products, when things need to be done, etc. Strategy for the entire company is focused on delivering new products on time and meeting quality, cost, and price targets while achieving research and development and capital targets. Members of the teams responsible for those products focus on those goals.

Target costing places problem solving and cost planning up front in the design stages of a new product development cycle. The goals of target costing are to simultaneously achieve total customer satisfaction and to ensure profitability for the manufacturer. It has been applied with great success in assembly-oriented industries, but its use is not limited to this domain.

Spurred by new competition, the prestigious U.S. firm decided to overhaul its cost management, new product development, and manufacturing methods. Caterpillar developed and implemented new target setting techniques throughout the company.

Although the actual application of target costing may differ from company to company, there are three key characteristics common to many applications.

- It is used at the planning and design stages.
- It involves profit and cost planning, not cost control.
- It is used for controlling design specifications and influencing production techniques.

Caterpillar's Aurora, Illinois, plant exemplifies the company's target costing efforts. Here, some 3,000 employees manufacture wheel loaders and excavators, which are distributed and sold competitively throughout the world.

Caterpillar's Business Environment

At Caterpillar, the need to continue to enhance target costing techniques was driven by a number of factors, including the company's emphasis on:

- providing outstanding customer service;
- meeting the competition's high-quality, low-cost product innovations;
- developing new manufacturing strategies;
- focusing on quality in terms of competitive designs as well as ongoing product and process improvements;
- creating new relationships with suppliers; and
- implementing changes throughout the company in every area from managerial perceptions to understanding the value of data and information in running the business.

In the process, Caterpillar expanded its emphasis on target costing to include achieving return on investment goals, targeting capital investment levels, and improving supplier alliances and engineering commitments. In the process, Caterpillar introduced a new way of thinking and reshaped corporate culture.

New product introduction became essential to Caterpillar's long-term strategy. New products and major updates to existing products now occur about every three years. Such changes are planned and coordinated within a nine-year planning horizon and driven by the new product managers, who incorporate changes in customer expectations and competitive pressures into new products. Important elements that influence price, profit, and cost are illustrated at the top of Exhibit 16–4.

Exhibit 16–4

The Target Costing Process

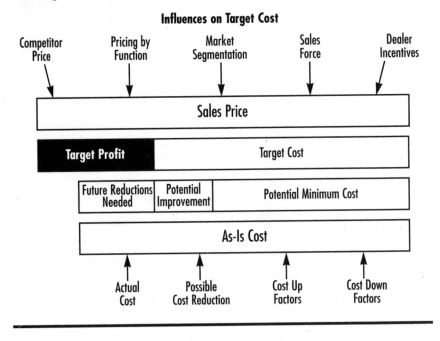

Influences on Target Cost

| Competitor Price | Pricing by Function | Market Segmentation | Sales Force | Dealer Incentives |

Sales Price

| Target Profit | Target Cost |

| Future Reductions Needed | Potential Improvement | Potential Minimum Cost |

As-Is Cost

| Actual Cost | Possible Cost Reduction | Cost Up Factors | Cost Down Factors |

Target Costing Implementation Issues

One of the critical issues the company faced in breaking with tradition was how to decompose target costs (see Exhibit 16–4). For example, in building an earth mover, the planners had to determine how much of the total cost should be designated for the drive train, the hydraulic, or any other particular part. Planners looked at these proportional costs as a study of major functions across product lines to find the best engineering solutions.

As it sought best-design solutions, Caterpillar management took this idea a step further. In addition to creating multi-functional product development teams, the company also organized specialty teams across product lines. The specialty teams focused on particular function and feature aspects of products. Because design decisions can influence a significant percentage of the total cost of a product, Caterpillar set up joint meetings in which these groups could exchange ideas and talk about design elements across product lines. A key focus was providing additional value at reduced cost.

Individuals throughout the organization working with the products also had to be kept fully informed about the overall project. They needed to understand that all members are part of a cross-functional team that designs, builds, develops, and decides on changes for various products.

Another Caterpillar innovation was the integration of strategic business objectives with quality function deployment (a method that systematically identifies and assigns relative weights of interest to different features or functions in products). Relative weights provide the indicators for determining where to spend time designing better features and implementing the features customers really want in their products.

Cost ownership, assigning responsibility for expenditures to those who actually do the work, is another key element of Caterpillar's successful cost management program. Accountability and cost ownership are assigned to the lowest possible levels of an organization. In the deployment of cost ownership and cost management objectives, the company spends hundreds of hours making sure everyone understands the importance of cost management; for example, the company provides regular training programs.

Conflict Between Cost Control and Product Cost Allocation

Creation of cost ownership has been an important innovation for Caterpillar in overcoming the traditional conflict between cost control and product cost allocation.

"Of late years, a great deal of accounting literature has been devoted to the philosophy of allocating overhead costs by point of contact," wrote Tom Sexton, Business Analysis Manager for Caterpillar's Aurora facility. "It has been properly stated that if accounting statements are to be used as tools for cost control, costs must be shown on these statements as chargeable to the individual who has control over the expenditure.

"This philosophy can be in direct conflict with a second and also important accounting function: determination of product costs. The determination of proper product costs requires the allocation of overhead costs by the type of plant activity causing the expenditure and this is often not the point of control.

"The conflicts can be easily illustrated by considering the expenses of the service departments, such as the maintenance department. Allocation by point of control of the wages paid maintenance personnel requires that these wages be shown on the expense statement of the head of the maintenance department to whom the mechanics report. On the other hand, allocation of these wages for determination of product costs would require that they be assigned, if not directly to the product being maintained, at least to the areas in which the maintenance personnel are working."

Five Essential Process Elements

Caterpillar's target costing process has five key elements:

- **target cost establishment:** satisfying customer needs and achieving enterprise financial goals;
- **cost management organization:** cost ownership and commitment by those who do the work;
- **cost management communication:** frequent management communication and education;
- **target cost maintenance:** negotiation and adjustment by cost owners; and
- **access to cost and target cost data:** finance provides financial analysis; current historical and projected costs for in-plant and out-plant suppliers through the business analysis function.

Caterpillar's Results

For Caterpillar, one important benefit of target costing is that it links product programs with the goals of the enterprise. It includes risk assessment, competitive analysis, and analysis of price/value/cost; establishes up-front accountability and cost ownership; and emphasizes profit planning and cost planning prior to production. Products are evaluated in terms of profit and cost targets over their entire life cycle.

The company leverages many factory and business systems as its primary source of data collection. Transactions that are gathered on the shop floor support financial accounting needs and some cost management requirements. The transactions are used to populate several databases simultaneously to provide the appropriate information to each user.

With the goal in mind of preserving cost competitiveness, target costs may be adjusted over time as the result of inflationary pressures. Target costs may also be normalized over multiyear windows for volume variances, exchange rate changes, and enterprise-level costs, so that fluctuations in these variables do not create unusual swings in target costs. Normalized period costs in the cost management database are compared during the production phase to normalized targets to evaluate progress on continuous cost reduction efforts.

LESSONS LEARNED

- Target costing is a competitive and strategic weapon.
- The target costing process requires managers to go beyond delegating responsibility to lead the company.
- Target costing requires cost awareness, cost accountability, and cost ownership on the part of everyone in the firm.
- Target costing requires a method for generating the kind of information necessary for managing the target costing processes. Targets can and should be established for all facets of a business, whether service organizations or products.
- Target costing is essentially a process to simultaneously achieve customer satisfaction and profitability.
- From a design goal objective, target costing looks simultaneously at managing quality, cost, and timing.

NOTE: Reid Dalton and Joe McNeely, Senior Managers with Arthur Andersen LLP in Chicago, are working with Caterpillar in designing and implementing a cost management system.

17

REPORTING ABC INFORMATION: ASKING THE RIGHT QUESTIONS GETS YOU TO THE RIGHT ANSWERS

CATHIE WIER AND BILLIE GAYLE LEWIS

Cathie Wier is a Senior Manager with Arthur Andersen LLP in San Jose.
Billie Gayle Lewis is a Senior Manager with Arthur Andersen LLP in Dallas.

"BEGIN WITH THE END IN MIND."
—Stephen R. Covey
Seven Habits of Highly Effective People

The success of every activity-based project, whether it is a pilot or a fully integrated implementation, rests on the information obtained from the model and how that information is used. Reports are the vehicle through which the information and insights gained from the project are conveyed to others. Thoughtful analysis leads to good reports, which lead, in turn, to action. Unless it flows this way, ABC is little more than an academic exercise.

Stacks of reports can be created from any model, but generating standard reports merely transforms data inputs into more data. Those pages and pages will document the model and list the costs of resources, activities, products, customers, services, etc. But is all of it really useful for decision making? Maybe. Good reports based in activity data, on the other hand, offer an understanding of the complex relationships buried in the company, which yields interpretations and conclusions. Good reports answer the questions that were raised when the long-ago decision to launch the project was made. Good reports test the original premise.

There is no standardized set of reports that can be used for all activity-based projects, so beginning with the end in mind, as Stephen Covey says, means that the time to address reporting needs is at the very beginning. The reports must take shape based on the organization's ABM goals and the decisions it will make using activity-based data.

If analysis and reports are planned at the outset of the project, sorting through the data when it is available will be much easier. The focus should be on analysis first. Reports constructed to represent the data or dynamic, on-line tools can be built in to allow others to work their way through the data. This chapter discusses how to report ABC information and how to avoid the pitfalls discussed in Exhibit 17–1.

Exhibit 17–1

Pitfalls Encountered When Reporting Activity-Based Data

Pitfall #1 Too much detail in a report makes conclusions and decisive action difficult.

Pitfall #2 Too little information may not be meaningful unless it is organized and presented in response to specific questions.

Pitfall #3 If sufficient supporting information does not accompany a report, resulting interpretations are likely to be faulty and actions taken ill-advised.

STRATEGIC VERSUS
OPERATIONAL REPORTS

There are two general categories of issues that are addressed in activity-based models: strategic and operational. Strategic and operational decision making require different levels of analysis and, consequently, different types of reports.

Strategic reports are conceptual and forward-looking; they help companies make strategic decisions about changing the ways they do business. Strategic reports deal with improvements in areas such as product mixes, customer and product margins, competitive positions and issues such as make versus buy analyses. Operational reports are more detailed and provide extensive activity information; they are used by line managers to analyze processes and highlight improvement opportunities. Although analysis of an activity-based model is simpler when only one of these categories is addressed, it is becoming more common to attempt to build a model that simultaneously addresses both some strategic and some operational analysis goals.

For example, Hewlett Packard's North American Distribution Organization (HP–NADO) wanted its model to address a broad set of strategic and operational issues (see Exhibit 17–2). Once they were defined, it was possible for the ABM implementation team to ask specific questions that related to each issue. These questions became the basis for decision making during the model-building phase, and were key when analysis of the models began.

Exhibit 17-2

Uses of the HP–NADO Model

Strategic
- Analyzing customer and channel profitability
- Supporting analysis of the contract discount structure
- Analyzing cost of key services provided
- Determining the impact of outsourcing distribution
- Supporting benchmark analysis of key areas
- Supporting investment justification decisions

Operational
- Supporting operational improvement teams
- Supporting activity-based budgeting/flexible budgeting
- Providing linkage to budgeting process
- Helping determine manager performance related to cost efficiency

STRATEGIC MODEL
REPORTS IN-DEPTH INFORMATION

A model built for strategic purposes is, typically, built to address issues such as product, service, or customer profitability, target costing, and make versus buy decisions. Analysis is typically focused on costs and profitability, rather than on details of operational performance. Consequently, certain types of comparisons, and even specific types of charts and graphs, are suggested.

Simple reports of strategic data are not necessarily all that will be needed. Managers must decide precisely what questions need to be answered related to each area and what level of detail will be useful. One report may show an over-all picture of product costs, for example, but reports focusing on specific comparisons will be needed in order to use the information effectively.

Product Cost

Product cost (see Exhibit 17–3) is a basic issue addressed by activity-based mod-els. A simple bar graph is used to show results as an alternate to the tabular view typically used to show results of the model.

Exhibit 17–3

Product Unit Cost

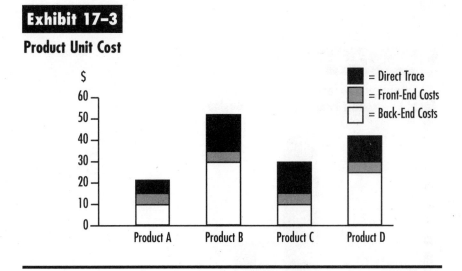

Combining this view with other data will show their relationships. This combined view of cost data can provide more valuable information than if pre-sented alone. But in order to determine what relationships will lead to a better understanding of costs, detailed questions must be asked:

- What is the service cost per net sales dollar produced?
- What is our cost compared to the cost for our competitors?
- What is the cost if we purchase components instead of producing them?
- What should our cost be?
- What are our margins by customer for these products?
- Can we increase margins? How?

Determining which questions need to be answered for decision making and subsequent action is the job of those implementing the project. Once the questions are determined, the analysis and related reports that are necessary can be specified.

Because of the large number of products involved at HP–NADO, reporting on each of the products in detail in one graph or table would have been overwhelming. Instead, when the company's ABM model was developed, products were grouped first by family; details of the product families could then be analyzed (see Exhibit 17–4). This level of detail not only shows the cost comparison of the product families, but begins to unravel the large differences in cost components for each product family.

Exhibit 17-4

HP Computer Products Distribution
Costs by Product Family (Supplies Business)

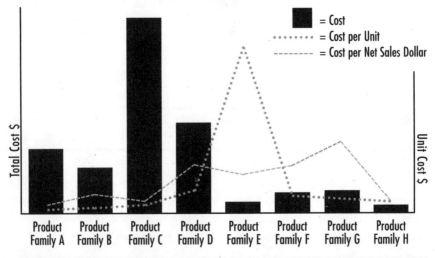

Product/Service Profitability

By comparing the profits of various products or product lines using a diagram similar to the costing chart shown below, it is easy to report on a company's product or service profitability (see Exhibit 17–5).

Exhibit 17–5

Total Product Profitability (000s)

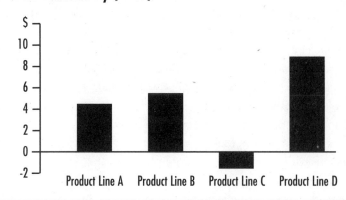

Is this information sufficient for decision making? Probably not. Imagine if a company made 500 products; what would a graph like this reveal? Not much more than raw data. To reveal more about the products in relation to each other, the data can be grouped and broken down to include the details of product cost and revenue that make up the profitability view (see Exhibit 17–6).

Exhibit 17–6

Average Unit Revenue/Cost/Profit

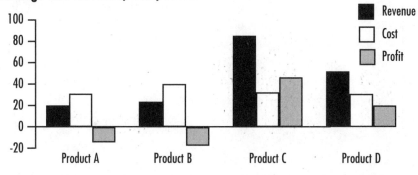

From a chart like the one in Exhibit 17–6, some of the differences between the products can be seen. If a high-priced product is not as profitable as expected, it is time to start analyzing why there is a discrepancy. But more powerful information is still needed. Before generating any reports, the analysis must be carefully considered:

- How should the data be ordered or grouped?
- How should the data be displayed (graph, chart, series)?
- Given the results, what follow-up questions will be asked?

The first two questions focus on organizational methods of interpreting information. The third focuses on digging deeper into the data. Is overall product performance and how the products contribute to the company's profitability truly the issue? Or is the goal to find out which products are unprofitable and why? Don't stop with simple answers. Continue to ask why, and truly understand the relationships. For many, when reviewing activity-based results for the first time, costs seem out of line. Making sure that analysis is sufficient to satisfy critical questions of data reliability is essential.

In most companies, there are several ways to analyze product profitability: by target market, price, manufacturing process, etc. It is important to understand and analyze the relationships of products in these categories as the profitability profile is interpreted.

At HP–NADO, product profitability was a primary strategic goal. Yet the focus of ABM reports was not on the profitability of each product. The focus was, rather, understanding the components of cost for each product family (see Exhibit 17–4, above).

Another way to add more information to a graph is to overlay different interpretations. For example, the addition of a cumulative profitability curve to a graph of individual products' profitability shows more clearly the effect the unprofitable products have on the overall profitability of the company (see Exhibit 17–7). Then, analysis could probe further to find out what is contributing to the cost of the unprofitable products. Are these low-volume products, or are there other reasons for their relatively poor performance?

If the data is available, it might be worthwhile to look at profitability trends as well. Which products are going up in cost, revenue, or margin? Which ones are going down? How does this affect the overall profitability curve and company interpretation of market opportunities?

Exhibit 17-7

Cumulative and Individual Product Profitability

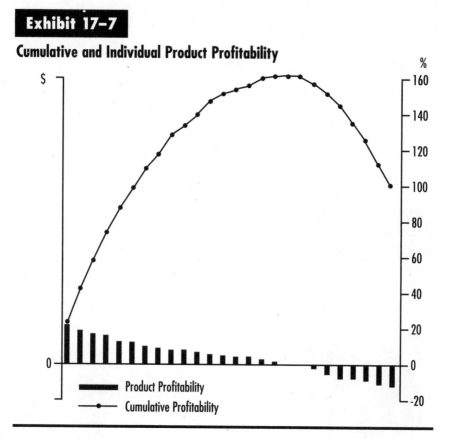

Product Profitability

Cumulative Profitability

Customer Profitability

Many of the same types of graphs can be used to depict the profitability of services, customers, and distribution channels. Just as some products contribute more to the profitability of a company, so do some customer segments.

In addition to customer profitability analyses, many companies today carefully review the interaction between products or services and customers. Instead of centering solely on unprofitable customers, it is possible to direct analysis to focus on the profitable customers, discovering what is going right. What is it about these customers that makes them profitable? Is it the combination of products that they buy, the distribution channels they purchase through, the quantities they purchase? Is it the fact that they buy electronically or require little or no support services? Once this composite of information is understood, the potential to enhance the appropriate market areas and, perhaps, increase the profitability in other customer segments becomes available.

An even more challenging perspective results from looking at the interrelationships among customer and product costs using activity-based analysis. The Slice & Dice Cube (see Chapter 4, Exhibit 4–1) is HP–NADO's depiction of this approach. The cube clarifies the relationships among products, customers, and the activities carried out to produce these products and provide these services to customers. It also provides the full set of information required for drill down, helping the company analyze profitability in a variety of ways. Exhibit 17–8 shows the cost component breakout for an individual customer and begins the drill down.

Exhibit 17–8

HP–NADO Computer Products Distribution Customer Cost Component Breakout

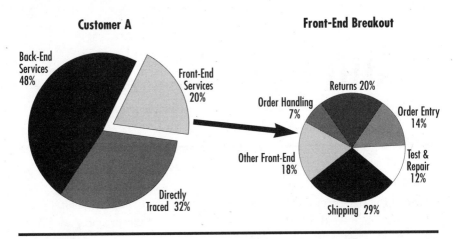

Customer A

- Back-End Services 48%
- Front-End Services 20%
- Directly Traced 32%

Front-End Breakout

- Returns 20%
- Order Handling 7%
- Order Entry 14%
- Other Front-End 18%
- Test & Repair 12%
- Shipping 29%

Focused Reports

In addition to producing cost and profitability reports, most strategic models lead to more specific analysis and related reports that focus on specific decisions and action. For example, an ABC model provides a natural lead-in to supporting target costing. Since the model holds detailed data about the cost components of a product (bill of activities, bill of resources, bill of materials), targets can be set to drive cost reduction efforts in each contributing area. Target cost reports compare actuals to target costs on a component basis; these smaller component targets are actionable. Successful steps in reaching the component targets combine to progress toward reaching the target costs of products.

OPERATIONAL MODEL
REPORTS IN-DEPTH INFORMATION

A model built for operational analysis is quite different from one used for strategic decision making. The operational model is more detailed in its activity and process analysis and may contain little or no analysis of products, customers, or other cost objects. The goals of an operational model are to understand activities and processes, reduce costs, improve quality, compress throughput time, and/or improve productivity. To achieve these goals, operational reports often use attribute flags such as value- or non-value-added, mission critical items, and cost-of-quality designations (including ISO-9000 clauses). Grouping activities in this way allows analysis of these categories, with both summary and detailed information available as needed.

The crossover between the strategic and operational view is the analysis of how the activities or processes contribute to a diverse set of products, services, customers, or other cost objects. For example, activities may be performed to meet the unique requirements of one or two specialty products or services. For strategic purposes, it is important to understand the additional cost of such activities and the effects on margin. For operational considerations, it is important to review these activities and to understand their value contribution and their overall effect on process efficiency. Sometimes it is precisely these activities that add value; sometimes the activities have evolved over time because of compromises in the process but add no value at all.

The typical questions to be answered in operational models are:

- How well are we performing our activities?
- What drives the cost of the significant activities?
- Which processes should we focus on for improvement efforts?
- What activities within those processes should be investigated?
- What areas require reengineering?
- What performance measures will focus workers on appropriate decisions?

These questions can be answered on several levels. But, when designing reports, it is important to remember which questions are critical. Since there are many ways to analyze activity information, decide what the important relationships are and begin there.

In operational analysis, pie charts are often used to show how activities or process costs contribute to overall costs (see Exhibit 17–9). At HP–NADO, detailed activity analysis was used to focus reengineering efforts in three pilot areas.

The first pie chart shows the cost of each activity in the front-end services

Exhibit 17-9

HP–NADO Order Entry Activity Decomposition

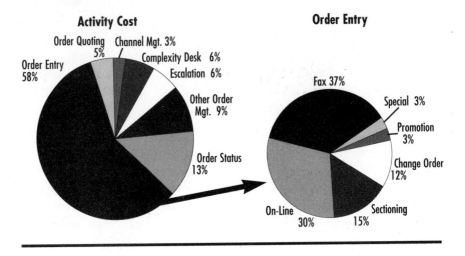

process. Because order entry is such a large component of overall process cost, it is appropriate to drill down further and understand the detailed activities that comprise it. Providing such detail makes it possible to understand specifically what improvement efforts can be undertaken.

Reports and graphs that detail long lists of activities and the percentage contribution of each activity to an equally long list of products, with lots of variability between products, can be generated. But what do they reveal? Simply that there is great variability in how products consume activities.

In this case, instead of looking at the details, it helps to start analysis at a high level with broad questions that can be answered. Then, it is fruitful to analyze the data in more detail. For example, start with process contribution, then for selected processes, drill down to more detailed analysis. The HP–NADO cube (see Chapter 4,.Exhibit 4–1) shows the variety of ways that information can be analyzed for operational understanding.

Operational models often lead to cross-functional and cross-process analysis. For example, a company may be interested in the cost of quality. In an ABM model appropriate activities can be tagged with a "quality" attribute. Resulting reports might include total cost of quality or more detailed analyses. For example, quality activities might be further designated as either proactive (prevention and appraisal) or reactive (internal and external failure) (see Exhibit 17–10).

Exhibit 17-10

Cost of Quality

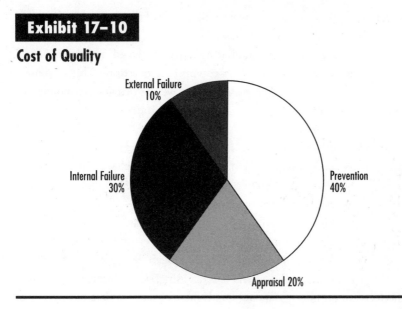

External Failure
10%

Internal Failure
30%

Prevention
40%

Appraisal 20%

Cross-functional analysis is especially useful when assessing operations. For example, the question, "How can we improve operations?," is too broad and can quickly lead to "analysis paralysis," the practice of analyzing and reporting information with no apparent purpose. Focused questions, which could lead to improved operations might include:

- What are our highest costs, non-value added activities?
- What drives the cost of these activities?

Operational analysis naturally leads to more than just cost information. For instance, performance management requires assessment of additional nonfinancial measures. Reports detailing their correlation with financial measures help managers understand whether the correct behaviors are being rewarded and whether balances are being achieved between performance objectives such as cycle time, quality, and cost.

LOOKING AHEAD

Conventional paper reports are no longer the only way to present information. On-line reporting is an alternative to, or at least an extension of, paper reporting. American Express, for instance, uses no paper reports in its ABM implementation. Instead, managers developed an on-line system for drilling down, asking questions, and getting information from the activity-based model. The system includes both strategic and operational views of the data, and all printed reports come straight from the on-line system.

As companies become more familiar with activity-based models, managers are realizing that the models can answer complicated questions. This awareness results in more detailed and complex models, as well as demand for more complex analysis and reports. Typically, the more useful the information generated from the model, the more new requests for information there are. The users of an ABM model represent many levels and functional areas of an organization. Each has a different viewpoint and requires a different level of detail and analysis to support their decisions. The volume of reports required to represent the variety of demand could be overwhelming.

Heavy demand for information is a sign of project success. But limiting fulfillment of that demand to an analyst only presents barriers between users with questions and the model that holds the answers. Although development of a direct-access, on-line reporting/analysis tool takes planning, organization, and training, the benefits of an on-line system and hands-on access to the data for individual analysis can be significant. (There are many on-line reporting tools on the market today. Options range from simple databases to decision support and executive information system applications that allow access to activity-based models.)

When a system is built effectively, users can investigate the model employing familiar terminology, ask high-level questions, and then drill down for more details. Allowing users to work with the information and find their own answers not only eliminates the bottleneck a dedicated report generator can represent, but also allows individuals to discover relationships in the data of which they might otherwise have been unaware. In addition, since all users are looking at data based on the same sources, the decisions they make are likely to be consistent.

LESSONS LEARNED

- Before starting a report, know what to look for, what questions to answer, and what decisions will be made from the information. Begin with the end in mind.
- A report needs to reveal information, not just data.
- A report should show or interpret conclusions or highlight the conclusions to be drawn from the data.
- Plan reporting from the outset of the project. This makes it easier to sort through the data as it becomes available.
- Consider on-line information analysis rather than printed reports.

WHAT THE FUTURE HOLDS

The field of activity-based management continues to grow. As it does, there will be many more lessons to learn. As they are learned, victories and success stories will continue to multiply.

Implementors will increasingly integrate ABM as a management strategy. It will be linked as an enabler to improvement efforts. As we have seen at AT&T and are seeing at the Covey Leadership Center, ABM will be integrated with the culture of the companies deploying it. ABM will be seen as a key way to understand and manage businesses on a process basis.

Academics have begun the transition to teaching ABM. However, in many cases, the material taught lags behind current practices. We hope this material helps improve the understanding of what leading edge companies are actually doing.

As ABM continues to mature, the role for consultants will certainly change. As the supply of experienced implementors grows, the need for basic ABM consulting will diminish. This will be replaced by demand for deeper, more advanced skills. This is evident in the Consortium for Advanced Manufacturing–International's (CAM–I) continuing research into areas such as capacity management, target costing, and understanding of process-based management.

Joe Donnelly of Arthur Andersen chairs CAM–I's Capacity Management Interest Group that is publishing a Capacity Management Primer. Tom Freeman of GTE heads CAM–I's Process-Based Management Group that will complete a Design Guidebook by the end of 1995. John Dutton of Arthur Andersen leads CAM–I's Target Costing Interest Group that plans to publish a Target Costing Primer in the Spring 1996. These developments will push ABM to deeper use in the management of companies.

Benchmarking remains a key tool in expanding our knowledge of what weapons companies use to successfully implement ABM. The American Productivity and Quality Center (APQC) joined CAM–I in completing a benchmarking study of the best practices in ABM. This landmark study, led by John Miller of Arthur Andersen, surveyed more than 700 companies with 150-plus responding as best practices companies. From the tabular survey, 30 detailed site visits were conducted. A second phase of research is beginning to more closely examine specific implementation tools such as training programs, organizational structures, reporting methods, and model support materials. The lessons from this research will dramatically improve the speed and effort needed to achieve an integrated roll-out.

ABM is a management tool that enables you to be a leader and a doer. These lessons are intended to help you avoid the pitfalls and to use the approaches that have led others to success. If by chance you fall into one of these pitfalls, use the recommended treatment alternatives to recover and move forward. If you find new pitfalls, share your findings. It will help everyone to better understand the ABM battlefield.

Victory belongs only to those bold enough to compete. We look forward to seeing you on the winning side.

APPENDIX I: PITFALLS ENCOUNTERED (WITH TRANSLATIONS) WHEN LAUNCHING AN ABM SYSTEM

Getting Off to the Right Start

WHAT THEY SAID	WHAT THEY MEANT
1 "We can't get the top guys to buy it."	Lack of Top Management Buy-In
2 "Okay, tell me again why we're doing this."	Lack of Clear Objectives
3 "What do you mean, there are three views of cost?"	Failure to Understand the Three Views of Costs
4 "Let's put the controller in charge."	Financial Person Heading the Project
5 "We'll tell the employees about this later — maybe."	Lack of Employee Involvement
6 "We can do this without spending any money."	Lack of Monetary Support
7 "We don't need training—this isn't brain surgery."	Lack of Training
8 "It's the consultant's fault."	Consultant Did Everything
9 "We don't need resident experts."	Lack of Cost Management Expertise
10 "This doesn't link to other initiatives."	Not Linking ABM with Other Initiatives

Developing the Pilot

WHAT THEY SAID	WHAT THEY MEANT
11 "Pilot? We don't need a pilot."	Failure to Do a Pilot First
12 "This thing needs a lot of detail."	Too Much Detail
13 "This thing doesn't need detail."	Too Little Detail
14 "What are you calling an activity?"	Problems in Collecting Activity Data
15 "That activity can't cost that much."	Inaccurate Assignment of Costs
16 "We don't keep data that way."	Unavailability of Detailed Data
17 "I think we spent that back in '62."	Assignment of Costs to the Wrong Year
18 "Who picked this software anyway?"	Software Problems
19 "Who needs project management?"	Poor Project Management
20 "I never dreamed it would take this long."	People Do Not Have Enough Time

Moving from Pilot to Mainstream

WHAT THEY SAID	WHAT THEY MEANT
21 "I'm afraid, but I don't know it."	Individual Resistance Due to Fear
22 "We're afraid, but we don't know it."	Departmental Resistance to Change
23 "Wait a minute—this is messing with some long-held beliefs."	People's Resistance to Changing Their Beliefs and Value Systems
24 "What a world."	Environmental Barriers to Change
25 "Oh, yeah, do something with the numbers."	Plans to Act on the Numbers Were Never Formalized
26 "Who wrote this, the legal department?"	Lack of Understandable Reports
27 "We were supposed to get this report two months ago."	Problems with Reporting Frequency
28 "They're overhead."	Not a Profit Center
29 "Times are good—why bother?"	Company is Too Profitable
30 "This will cost a fortune to operate."	ABM Is Too Costly to Maintain

APPENDIX II:
ACTIVITY-BASED COSTING CRITERIA FOR SELECTING SUCCESSFUL PILOT SITES

The following is a list of criteria that should be considered when selecting a successful pilot site. Apparent redundancies are intentional and facilitate a multidimensional review of the site's readiness for quantifying its cost structure.

Categories
The list is broken into seven categories: Strategy; Process; Technology; People; Results; Focus; and Scope/Scale.

Importance Ranking
Use a weighting factor of 1 to 5 (5 being most important to the company) to rank the importance of the criteria being considered.

Presence of Condition
For criteria, circle the appropriate symbol:
- ● (Yes)   the condition/requirement exists at the site;
- ✪ (Partially) the condition/requirement partially exists at the site;
- ○ (No)   the condition/requirement does not exist at the site.

The sites selected should have the most criteria met with the highest weighted scores.

Potential Site _____

	Importance Rank (5 most important) 1-5 / A	Presence of Condition (5) Yes	(3) Partially	(1) No / B	Score A x B
1. Strategy					
A. Local project management support	____	●	✪	○	____
B. Understands customer needs	____	●	✪	○	____
C. Understands internal/external competition	____	●	✪	○	____
D. Coverage—commercial market	____	●	✪	○	____
E. Coverage—defense market	____	●	✪	○	____
F. Product coverage—assembly	____	●	✪	○	____
G. Product coverage—components	____	●	✪	○	____
H. Service coverage—shared services (i.e., MIS)	____	●	✪	○	____
I. Product diversity/complexity exists	____	●	✪	○	____
J. Ready to make tough decisions/ready to change	____	●	✪	○	____
Subtotal					____

	Importance Rank (5 most important) 1-5 A	Yes (5)	Partially (3)	No (1)	Score A x B

2. Process

	Importance Rank ___ A	Yes ●	Partially ✪	No ○	Score ___
A. Understands critical business processes	___	●	✪	○	___
B. Ability to focus on future cost targets	___	●	✪	○	___
C. Potential constraints or excess capacities	___	●	✪	○	___
D. Information on key activities by process	___	●	✪	○	___
E. Simultaneously focusing on quality, cost, and timing	___	●	✪	○	___
F. Understands customer service/profitability priorities	___	●	✪	○	___
Subtotal					___

3. Technology

		Yes ●	Partially ✪	No ○	Score ___
A. Capacity can be measured and information is available	___	●	✪	○	___
B. Key Volume information is available	___	●	✪	○	___
C. Operating systems are reliable and accessible	___	●	✪	○	___
D. Not tainted by prior "one-time" studies	___	●	✪	○	___
E. Ability to visualize strategic, operational, and financial views of cost	___	●	✪	○	___
F. Decision makers want information	___	●	✪	○	___
G. System support personnel are available for volume information	___	●	✪	○	___
H. Operating in "Windows" environment	___	●	✪	○	___
Subtotal					___

4. People

		Yes ●	Partially ✪	No ○	Score ___
A. Dedicated champion(s) is/are available	___	●	✪	○	___
B. Operations personnel are available to support pilot	___	●	✪	○	___
C. Team members understand business operations	___	●	✪	○	___
D. Cross-functional team to support the project	___	●	✪	○	___
E. Team can focus on analytical reporting and "process" thinking	___	●	✪	○	___
F. Dedicated, motivated, and near full-time team	___	●	✪	○	___
G. Ability to train and follow through	___	●	✪	○	___
H. Union receptivity to quantifying unit costs	___	●	✪	○	___
Subtotal					___

	Importance Rank (5 most important) 1-5 A	Presence of Condition (5) Yes	(3) Partially	(1) No	Score A x B

5. Results: Identify and quantify the following benefits areas:

	A	Yes	Partially	No	A x B
A. Hidden operational complexity costs	____	●	✪	○	____
B. Potential unprofitable products or processes	____	●	✪	○	____
C. Cost of unused/idle capacity	____	●	✪	○	____
D. "True" cost of outsourcing rather than producing	____	●	✪	○	____
E. Opportunities for process support-cost reduction	____	●	✪	○	____
F. Manufacturing cost of quality	____	●	✪	○	____
G. Cost targets for interplant benchmarking	____	●	✪	○	____
Subtotal					____

6. Focus: Operationally review the following:

	A	Yes	Partially	No	A x B
A. Partnership opportunities with customers, suppliers	____	●	✪	○	____
B. Efficient new product development	____	●	✪	○	____
C. Critical opportunities to improve processes	____	●	✪	○	____
D. Reducing overall complexity in the business	____	●	✪	○	____
E. Output and process performance measures	____	●	✪	○	____
F. Customer satisfaction links to processes	____	●	✪	○	____
G. Cost management links to processes	____	●	✪	○	____
H. Continuous improvement of unit costs	____	●	✪	○	____
Subtotal					____

7. Scope/Scale

	A	Yes	Partially	No	A x B
A. Management business issues are identified	____	●	✪	○	____
B. Diversity in products, processes, or customers	____	●	✪	○	____
C. Indirect costs are currently incurred at the site	____	●	✪	○	____
D. Indirect costs are currently allocated to the site	____	●	✪	○	____
E. Data is available to support the unit cost analysis	____	●	✪	○	____
F. Operational scenarios can be articulated	____	●	✪	○	____
G. Time frame of study is manageable	____	●	✪	○	____
H. Key success factors are identifiable	____	●	✪	○	____
I. Dedicated resources are available	____	●	✪	○	____
J. Lack of overriding global issues to cloud project	____	●	✪	○	____
Subtotal					____

SUMMARY
1. Strategy ____
2. Process ____
3. Technology ____
4. People ____
5. Results ____
6. Focus ____
7. Scope/Scale ____
TOTAL ____

Source: This checklist was initially prepared by Chuck Marx and Mike Retrum for an aerospace manufacturer. It is derived from an Arthur Andersen-Global Best Practice presentation titled "Best Practices in Activity-Based Costing" and an article titled "The Top 10 Things That Can Go Wrong With ABC Implementations" written by Steve Player and Chuck Marx.

STAGES OF COST AND PERFORMANCE
MEASUREMENT SYSTEMS DEVELOPMENT

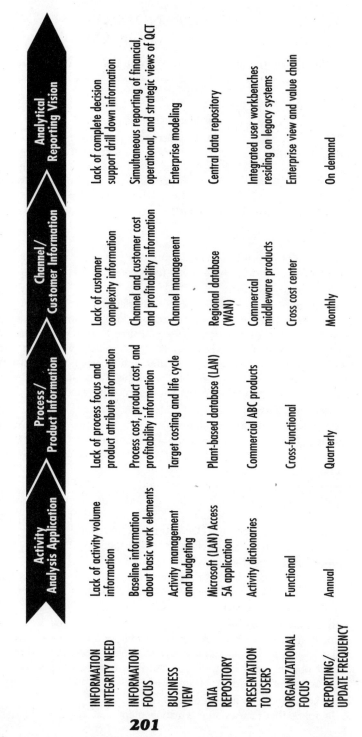

	Activity Analysis Application	Process/ Product Information	Channel/ Customer Information	Analytical Reporting Vision
INFORMATION INTEGRITY NEED	Lack of activity volume information	Lack of process focus and product attribute information	Lack of customer complexity information	Lack of complete decision support drill down information
INFORMATION FOCUS	Baseline information about basic work elements	Process cost, product cost, and profitability information	Channel and customer cost and profitability information	Simultaneous reporting of financial, operational, and strategic views of QCT
BUSINESS VIEW	Activity management and budgeting	Target costing and life cycle	Channel management	Enterprise modeling
DATA REPOSITORY	Microsoft (LAN) Access 5A application	Plant-based database (LAN)	Regional database (WAN)	Central data repository
PRESENTATION TO USERS	Activity dictionaries	Commercial ABC products	Commercial middleware products	Integrated user workbenches residing on legacy systems
ORGANIZATIONAL FOCUS	Functional	Cross-functional	Cross cost center	Enterprise view and value chain
REPORTING/ UPDATE FREQUENCY	Annual	Quarterly	Monthly	On demand

APPENDIX IV:
GLOSSARY OF TERMS

Note: All terms are taken directly from the CAM-I Glossary of Terms
Version 1.2 unless noted by an (*)

ABC* – See *activity-based costing.*

ABM* – See *activity-based management.*

ABO (Awareness, Buy-in, Ownership) ContinuumSM*
This tool, developed by Arthur Andersen, describes the process through which executives must move when implementing a change initiative. It is comprised of three phases: awareness (executives know something important is happening and they show interest in it), buy-in (executives move to personal involvement with the change initiative), and ownership (executives assume ultimate responsibility for making the change happen).

Activity
1. Work performed within an organization. 2. An aggregation of actions performed within an organization that is useful for purposes of activity-based costing.

Activity analysis
The identification and description of activities in an organization. Activity analysis involves determining what activities are done within a department, how many people perform the activities, how much time is spent performing the activities, what resources are required to perform the activities, what operational data best reflect the performance of the activities, and what value the activity has for the organization. Activity analysis is accomplished by means of interviews, questionnaires, observation, and review of physical records of work.

Activity attributes
Characteristics of individual activities. Attributes include cost drivers, cycle time, capacity, and performance measures. For example, a measure of the elapsed time required to complete an activity is an attribute. (See *cost driver* and *performance measures.*)

Activity-based budgeting*
A process by which a company uses its understanding of its activities and driver relationships to set better budgets. This is achieved by determining estimates of volume that drive activities. Determines activity levels that drive activity costs, and gives an entity greater ability to predict spending.

Activity-based cost system
A system that maintains and processes financial and operating data on a firm's resources, activities, cost objects, cost drivers, and activity performance measures. It also assigns costs to activities and cost objects.

Activity-based costing
A methodology that measures the cost and performance of activities, resources, and cost objects. Resources are assigned to activities, then activities are assigned to cost objects based on their use. Activity-based costing recognizes the causal relationships of cost drivers to activities.

Activity-based management
A discipline that focuses on the management of activities as the route to improv-

ing the value received by the customer and the profit achieved by providing this value. This discipline includes cost driver analysis, activity analysis, and performance measurement. Activity-based management draws on activity-based costing as its major source of information.

Activity cost assignment
The process through which costs of activities are attached to cost objects using activity drivers. (See *cost object* and *activity driver*.)

Activity cost pool
A grouping of all cost elements associated with an activity. (See *cost element*.)

Activity dictionary*
A listing of standardized definitions of common activities typically used in an activity-based analysis. Activities are defined as verb/noun such as "enter orders." Activity dictionaries often have a numbering and classification scheme.

Activity driver
A measure of the frequency and intensity of the demands placed on activities by cost objects. An activity driver is used to assign costs to cost objects. It represents a line item on the bill of activities for a product or customer. An example is the number of part numbers, which is used to measure the consumption of material-related activities by each product, material type, or component. The number of customer orders measures the consumption of order-entry activities by each customer. Sometimes an activity driver is used as an indicator of the output of an activity, such as the number of purchase orders prepared by the purchasing activity. (See *cost object* and *bill of activities*.)

Activity driver analysis
The identification and evaluation of the activity drivers used to trace the cost of activities to cost objects. Activity driver analysis may also involve selecting activity drivers with a potential for cost reduction.

Activity level
A description of how an activity is used by a cost object or other activity. Some activity levels describe the cost object that uses the activity and the nature of this use. These levels include activities that are traceable to the product (i.e., unit-level, batch-level, and product-level costs), to the customer (customer-level costs), to a market (market-level costs), to a distribution channel (channel-level costs), and to a project, such as a research and development project (project-level costs).

Allocation
1. An apportionment or distribution. 2. A process of assigning cost to an activity or cost object when a direct measure does not exist. For example, assigning the cost of power to a machine activity by means of machine hours is an allocation because machine hours are an indirect measure of power consumption. In some cases, allocations can be converted to tracings by incurring additional measurement costs. Instead of using machine hours to allocate power consumption, for example, a company can place a power meter on machines to measure actual power consumption. (See *tracing*.)

Assignment – See *cost assignment*.

Attribute flag*
A method of classifying activities that allows an entity to group related costs for better focus or analysis. Examples include value-added versus non-value added and

cost of quality such as preventive, internal failure, and external failure.

Attributes
Characteristics of activities, such as cost drivers and performance measures. (See *cost driver* and *performance measure*.)

Attribution – See *tracing*.

Benchmarking – See *best practices*.

Best practices
A methodology that identifies an activity as the standard, or benchmark, by which a similar activity will be judged. This methodology is used to assist in identifying a process or technique that can increase the effectiveness or efficiency of an activity. The source may be internal (e.g., taken from another part of the company) or external (e.g., taken from a competitor). Another term used is *competitive benchmarking*.

Bill of activities
A listing of the activities required (and, optionally, the associated costs of the resources consumed) by a product or other cost object.

Business process reengineering (BPR)*
An approach to improving the operations of a business that focuses on the horizontal process by which work is performed. This approach seeks a dramatic improvement through complete redesign (or reengineering) of the way the process is performed.

Competitive benchmarking – See *best practices*.

Consortium for Advanced Manufacturing–International* (CAM–I)
CAM–I, a not-for-profit membership organization that has been in existence for over 20 years, supports research and development in areas of strategic importance to the manufacturing industries. Since 1988, CAM–I's Cost Management System (CMS) Program—a coalition of members from industry, government, and academia—has been recognized internationally as the leading forum for the advancement of cost management research and practice.

Cost Accounting Standards
1. Rules promulgated by the Cost Accounting Standards Board (CASB) of the federal government to ensure contractor compliance in accounting for government contracts. 2. A set of rules issued by any of several authorized organizations or agencies, such as the American Institute of Certified Public Accountants (AICPA) or the Association of Chartered Accountants (ACA), dealing with the determination of costs to be allocated, inventoried, or expensed.

Cost assignment
The tracing or allocation of resources to activities or cost objects. (See *allocation* and *tracing*.)

Cost center
The basic unit of responsibility in an organization for which costs are accumulated.

Cost driver
Any factor that causes a change in the cost of an activity. For example, the quality of parts received by an activity (e.g., the percent that are defective) is a determining factor in the work required by that activity because the quality of parts received affects the resources required to perform the activity. An activity may have multiple cost drivers associated with it.

Cost driver analysis

The examination, quantification, and explanation of the effects of cost drivers. Management often uses the results of cost driver analyses in continuous improvement programs to help reduce throughput time, improve quality, and reduce cost. (See *cost driver* and *continuous improvement program.*)

Cost element

An amount paid for a resource consumed by an activity and included in an activity cost pool. For example, power cost, engineering cost, and depreciation may be cost elements in the activity cost pool for a machine activity. (See *activity cost pool* and *bill of activities.*)

Cost object

Any customer, product, service, contract, project, or other work unit for which a separate cost measurement is desired.

Cost of quality

All the resources expended for appraisal costs, prevention costs, and both internal and external failure costs of activities and cost objects.

Cost pool – See *activity cost pool.*

Direct cost

A cost that can be easily traced to an activity or a cost object. For example, the material issued to a particular work order and the engineering time devoted to a specific product are direct costs to the work orders or products. (See *tracing.*)

Drilling down*

The process of progressively analyzing cost detail starting at a high level and then going into the costs respective elements and components. Each level or layer of cost is examined in more granularity allowing greater understanding but typically at an increasing level of effort (and cost) in analyzing. The process should stop when the cost of going more detailed exceeds the value of the additional detail analyzed.

Financial view of cost*

This is one of the three primary views of cost. It represents the traditional approach to costing using the historical cost concept. It is typically used by financial controllers and tax managers to value inventory and report to shareholders, lenders, and tax authorities. This view is used in financial accounting and typically follows statutory reporting rules such as generally accepted accounting principals or tax regulations. Its focus is on the past. The measures used are nearly all financial.

Fixed cost

A cost element of an activity that does not vary with changes in the volume of cost drivers or activity drivers. The depreciation of a machine, for example, may be assigned to a particular activity, but it is fixed with respect to changes in the number of units of the activity driver. The designation of a cost element as fixed or variable may vary depending on the time frame of the decision in question and the extent to which the volume of production, activity drivers, or cost drivers changes.

Focus group*

A data collection method in which a group of individuals is surveyed together. This approach allows individual feedback and is more efficient in data collection due to the simultaneous data collection from a group.

Indirect cost
The cost that is allocated—as opposed to being traced—to an activity or a cost object. For example, the costs of supervision or heat may be allocated to an activity on the basis of direct labor hours. (See *allocation*.)

Just-in-Time training*
A training approach in which individuals are trained to perform necessary tasks immediately prior to performing them. This approach increases the likelihood of training retention due to its immediate application.

Life cycle – See *product life cycle*.

Non-value-added activity
An activity that is considered not to contribute to customer value or to the organization's needs. The designation "non-value-added" reflects a belief that the activity can be redesigned, reduced, or eliminated without reducing the quantity, responsiveness, or quality of the output required by the customer or the organization. (See *value analysis*.)

Operational view of cost*
This is one of the three primary views of cost. It represents the view of cost needed for a day-to-day cost management by line managers, process improvement teams, and quality teams. This cost information is used as an indicator of performance and to determine if activities are adding value. Its time focus is typically short-term with the need for immediate feedback. The measures used tend to be mostly physical.

Opportunity cost
The economic value of a benefit sacrificed when an alternative course of action is selected.

Performance measures
Indicators of the work performed and the results achieved in an activity, process, or organizational unit. Performance measures may be financial or nonfinancial. An example of a performance measure of an activity is the number of defective parts per million. An example of a performance measure of an organizational unit is return on sales.

Process
A series of activities that are linked to perform a specific objective. For example, the assembly of a television set or the paying of a bill or claim entails several linked activities.

Product life cycle
The period that starts with the initial product specification and ends with the withdrawal of the product from the marketplace. A product life cycle is characterized by defined stages, including research, development, introduction, maturity, decline, and abandonment.

Project costing
A cost system that collects information on activities and costs associated with a specific activity, project, or program.

Resource driver
A measure of the quantity of resources consumed by an activity. An example of a resource driver is the percentage of total square feet occupied by an activity. This fac-

tor is used to allocate a portion of the cost of operating the facility to the activity.

Rifle meeting*

A data collection method which is used to rapidly gather information. Under this approach managers gather to provide the requested data for an activity survey. This group meeting is held to explain forms and immediately gather the required information.

Roll out*

The steps to be taken in expanding the improvement effort from the pilot stage to full implementation.

Rolling up*

The summing up of lower level detail into higher aggregations such as in adding activity costs together to determine process costs.

Strategic view of cost*

This is one of the three primary views of cost. It represents the futuristic view of cost used by strategic planners, cost engineers and sales management to determine how to impact future costs and improve future profitability. This cost information is used to understand the cost of various cost objects such as products, customers, or channels. Its time focus is on the future using a combination of both physical and financial measures.

Support costs

Costs of activities not directly associated with production. Examples are the costs of process engineering and purchasing.

Surrogate activity driver

An activity driver that is not descriptive of an activity, but that is closely corre-lated to the performance of the activity. A surrogate activity driver should reduce measurement costs without significantly increasing the costing bias. The number of production runs is not descriptive of the material-disbursing activity, but the number of production runs may be used as an activity driver if material disburse-ments coincide with production runs.

Target cost

A cost calculated by subtracting a desired profit margin from an estimated (or a market-based) price to arrive at a desired production, engineering, or marketing cost. The target cost need not be the expected initial production cost. Instead, it may be the cost that is expected to be achieved during the mature production stage. (See *target costing*.)

Target costing

A method used in analyzing product and process design that involves estimating a target cost and designing the product to meet that cost. (See *target cost*.)

Throughput

The rate of production of a defined process over a stated period of time. Rates may be expressed in terms of units of products, batches produced, dollar turnover, or other meaningful measurements.

Time study*

A measurement process that is used to determine the amount of time spent per-forming individual activities. Typically used in establishing work standards, these measures are more accurate that using manager or worker time estimates, howev-er they are also more expensive to develop and maintain.

Total-quality management (TQM)*
Describes an approach to managing an enterprise that focuses on quality to achieve the desired results. Total-quality management focuses on meeting or exceeding the needs of customers as well as other stakeholders such as employees, owners and the community as a whole. Continuous improvement is a key element of this approach.

Traceability
The ability to assign a cost directly to an activity or a cost object in an economically feasible way by means of a causal relationship. (See *tracing*.)

Tracing
The assignment of cost to an activity or a cost object using an observable measure of the consumption of resources by an activity. Tracing is generally preferred to allocation if the data exist or can be obtained at a reasonable cost. For example, if a company's cost accounting system captures the cost supplies according to which activities use the supplies, the costs may be traced—as opposed to allocated—to the appropriate activities. Tracing is also called *direct tracing*.

Unit cost
The cost associated with a single unit of a product, including direct costs, indirect costs, traced costs, and allocated costs.

Value-added activity
An activity that contributes to customer value or satisfy an organizational need. "Value-added" reflects a belief that the activity cannot be eliminated without reducing the quantity, responsiveness, or quality of output required by a customer or organization.

Value analysis
A cost-reduction and process-improvement tool that utilizes information collected about business processes and examines various attributes of the processes (e.g., diversity, capacity, and complexity) to identify candidates for improvement efforts. (See *activity attributes* and *cost driver*.)

Variable cost
A cost element of an activity that varies with changes in volume of cost drivers and activity drivers. The cost of material handling to an activity, for example, varies according to the number of material deliveries and pickups to and from that activity. (See *cost element*, *fixed cost*, and *activity driver*.)

Waste
Resources consumed by unessential or inefficient activities.

Work center
A physical area of the plant or factory. It consists of one or more resources where a particular product or process is accomplished.

Note: Terms not indicated with an (*) were adapted with permission from the Consortium for Advanced Manufacturing–International (CAM–I) Cost Management System's Glossary of Terms. ©1991 CAM–I, Document #R-91-CMS-06, Version 1.2.

ABOUT THE EDITORS

Steve Player, CPA, is Partner and Firmwide Director of Cost Management at Arthur Andersen. He designs and implements advanced cost management programs for clients including Hewlett-Packard, NordicTrack, Texas Instruments, American Express, and Tyson Foods. He is Chairman of the CAM–I Cost Management System Program.

Steve leads Arthur Andersen's Advanced Cost Management Team (ACT). ACT is part of the Business Consulting practice, which assists companies in improving business processes and technologies through specialization in cost management, performance measures, reengineering, organizational improvement, and business systems consulting services. Linking the ABM Best Practices Study, led by Arthur Andersen's John Miller, with the Global Best Practices[SM] knowledge base, allows Arthur Andersen to deliver integrated business solutions to clients worldwide.

David E. Keys, CMA, CPA, is Household International Professor of Accountancy at Northern Illinois University. He writes for publications including *Management Accounting, Journal of Cost Management,* and *Accounting Review.* He has received several awards for excellence in teaching and has consulted with numerous companies.

To order additional copies of *Activity-Based Management: Arthur Andersen's Lessons from the ABM Battlefield,* send a check for $24.95 for each book ordered plus $2 postage and handling for the first book, and $1 for each additional copy to:

MasterMedia Limited
17 East 89th Street
New York, NY 10128
(212) 546-7650
(800) 334-8232; please use MasterCard or VISA on phone orders
(212) 546-7638 (fax)

Steve Player and David E. Keys are available for speaking engagements. Please contact MasterMedia's Speaker's Bureau for availability and fee arrangements. Call Tony Colao at (800) 453-2887.

OTHER MASTERMEDIA BUSINESS BOOKS

To order additional copies of any MasterMedia book, send a check for the price of the book plus $2.00 postage and handling for the first book, $1.00 for each additional book to:

MasterMedia Limited
17 East 89th Street
New York, NY 10128
(212) 260-5600
(800) 334-8232 please use MasterCard or VISA on 1-800 orders
(212) 546-7638 (fax)

BEYOND SUCCESS: How Volunteer Service Can Help You Begin Making a Life Instead of Just a Living, by John F. Raynolds III and Eleanor Raynolds, C.B.E., is a unique how-to book targeted at business and professional people considering volunteer work, senior citizens who wish to fill leisure time meaningfully, and students trying out various career options. The book is filled with interviews with celebrities, CEOs, and average citizens who talk about the benefits of service work. ($19.95 cloth)

BOUNCING BACK: How to Turn Business Crises Into Success, by Harvey Reese. Based on interviews with entrepreneurs from coast to coast, this fascinating book contains cautionary tales that unfold with gripping suspense. Reese has discovered a formula for success that should be "must reading" for every new or budding entrepreneur. ($18.95 hardbound)

DARE TO CHANGE YOUR JOB—AND YOUR LIFE, by Carole Kanchier, Ph.D., provides a look at career growth and development throughout the life cycle. ($9.95 paper)

HOW TO GET WHAT YOU WANT FROM ALMOST ANYBODY, by T. Scott Gross, shows how to get great service, negotiate better prices, and always get what you pay for. ($9.95 paper)

LIFETIME EMPLOYABILITY: How to Become Indispensable, by Carole Hyatt, is both a guide through the mysteries of the business universe brought down to earth and a handbook to help you evaluate your attitudes, your skills, and your goals. Through expert advice and interviews of nearly 200 men and women whose lives have changed because their jobs or goals shifted, *Lifetime Employability* is designed to increase your staying power in today's down-sized economy. ($12.95 paper)

LEADING YOUR POSITIVELY OUTRAGEOUS SERVICE TEAM, by T. Scott Gross, provides a step-by-step formula for developing self-managing, excited service teams that put the customer first. T. Scott Gross tackles the question businesses everywhere are asking: "How do I get ordinary people to give world-class service?" A must-have for creating tomorrow's corporation today! ($12.95 paper)

THE LOYALTY FACTOR: Building Trust in Today's Workplace, by Carol Kinsey Goman, Ph.D., offers techniques for restoring commitment and loyalty in the workplace. ($9.95 paper)

MANAGING IT ALL: Time-Saving Ideas for Career, Family, Relationships, and Self, by Beverly Benz Treuille and Susan Schiffer Stautberg, is written for women who are juggling careers and families. Over two hundred career women (ranging from a TV anchorwoman to an investment banker) were interviewed. The book contains many humorous anecdotes on saving time and improving the quality of life for self and family. ($9.95 paper)

OUT THE ORGANIZATION: New Career Opportunities for the 1990's, by Robert and Madeleine Swain, is written for the millions of Americans whose jobs are no longer safe, whose companies are not loyal, and who face futures of uncertainty. It gives advice on finding a new job or starting your own business. ($12.95 paper)

POSITIVELY OUTRAGEOUS SERVICE: New and Easy Ways to Win Customers for Life, by T. Scott Gross, identifies what the consumers of the nineties really want and how businesses can develop effective marketing strategies to answer those needs. ($14.95 paper)

POSITIVELY OUTRAGEOUS SERVICE AND SHOWMANSHIP: Industrial Strength Fun Makes Sales Sizzle!!!!, by T. Scott Gross, reveals the secrets of adding personality to any product or service. ($12.95 paper)

REAL LIFE 101: The Graduate's Guide to Survival, by Susan Kleinman, supplies welcome advice to those facing "real life" for the first time, focusing on work, money, health, and how to deal with freedom and responsibility. ($9.95 paper)

A SEAT AT THE TABLE: An Insider's Guide for America's New Women Leaders, by Patricia Harrison, provides practical and insightful advice for women who are interested in serving on a board of directors, playing a key role in politics and becoming a policy- or opinion-maker in public or private sectors. This is one book every woman needs to own. ($19.95 hardbound)

SIDE-BY-SIDE STRATEGIES: How Two-Career Couples Can Thrive in the Nineties, by Jane Hershey Cuozzo and S. Diane Graham, describes how two-career couples can learn the difference between competing with a spouse and becoming a supportive power partner. Published in hardcover as *Power Partners*. ($10.95 paper, $19.95 cloth)

STEP FORWARD: Sexual Harassment in the Workplace, What You Need to Know, by Susan L. Webb, presents the facts for identifying the tell-tale signs of sexual harassment on the job, and how to deal with it. ($9.95 paper)

TAKING CONTROL OF YOUR LIFE: The Secrets of Successful Enterprising Women, by Gail Blanke and Kathleen Walas, is based on the authors' professional experience with Avon Products' Women of Enterprise Awards, given each year to outstanding women entrepreneurs. The authors offer a specific plan to help women gain control over their lives, and include business tips and quizzes as well as beauty and lifestyle information. ($17.95 cloth)

TEAMBUILT: Making Teamwork Work, by Mark Sanborn, teaches business how to improve productivity, without increasing resources or expenses, by building teamwork among employers. ($19.95 cloth)

A TEEN'S GUIDE TO BUSINESS: The Secrets to a Successful Enterprise, by Linda Menzies, Oren S. Jenkins, and Rickell R. Fisher, provides solid information about starting your own business or working for one. ($7.95 paper)

TWENTYSOMETHING: Managing and Motivating Today's New Work Force, by Lawrence J. Bradford, Ph.D., and Claire Raines, M.A., examines the work orientation of the younger generation, offering managers in businesses of all kinds a practical guide to better understand and supervise their young employees. ($22.95 cloth)

WORK WITH ME: How to Make the Most of Office Support Staff, by Betsy Zazary, shows you how to find, train, and nurture the "perfect" assistant and how to best utilize your support staff professionals. ($9.95 paper)